ON-PURPOSE LEADERSHIP

Dale Galloway's years of experience as an effective pastor plus his ministry to hundreds of other pastors uniquely qualify him to write about the kind of spiritual leadership required to build a high-impact church.

—Bob Russell, Senior Minister, Southeast Christian Church, Louisville, Kentucky

The topics are practical, up-to-date, and biblical. He understands the importance of leadership in reaching lost people in the 21st century. This book may be his best book yet.

—Bob Huffaker, Senior Pastor, Grove City Church of the Nazarene, Grove City, Ohio

It is a manual you can refer to, a resource book to give to your leaders, and a check-up guide to examine your leadership motives and abilities.

—Billy Joe Daugherty, Senior Pastor, Victory Christian Center, Tulsa, Oklahoma

This is a very practical book for the leader and layperson alike. It will provide the knowledge needed to excel in church leadership.

—David Yonggi Cho, Senior Pastor, Yoido Full Gospel Central Church, Seoul, Korea

In this book Dale Galloway has distilled the wisdom not only of his own creative imagination in leadership but also of outstanding Christian leaders whose guidance he has tested in local congregations.

—Maxie D. Dunnam, President, Asbury Theological Seminary, Wilmore, Kentucky

Dale Galloway's whole life is about developing leaders for the purposes of God. This practical book will dramatically help thousands of other leaders do the same!

—Mike Breaux, Senior Minister, Southland Christian Church, Lexington, Kentucky

I enthusiastically recommend that *On-Purpose Leadership* be a "must read" for everyone committed to leading and building dynamic, devoted ministry as Jesus did.

—Walt Kallestad, Senior Pastor, Community Church of Joy, Glendale, Arizona

Dale Galloway shares from 30 years of practical experience the proven principles of leadership that he has successfully used. This book will doubtless become a leadership classic.

—Ray Cotton, Senior Pastor, New Hope Community Church, Portland, Oregon

ON

Multiplying Your Ministry by Becoming a Leader of Leaders

PURPOSE
LEADERSHIP

BY DALE E. GALLOWAY
WITH WARREN BIRD

Beacon Hill Press of Kansas City
Kansas City, Missouri

Some of this material originally appeared as articles in *Net Results* magazine, and is used by permission of Net Results, 5001 Ave. "N," Lubbock, TX 79412-2993; phone: 806-762-8094; fax: 806-762-8873; web site: www.netresults.org.

All Scripture quotations are taken from the *Holy Bible, New International Version®* (NIV®). Copyright © 1973, 1978, 1984 by International Bible Society. Used by permission of Zondervan Publishing House. All rights reserved.

Permission to quote from the following copyrighted versions of the Bible is acknowledged with appreciation:

The New English Bible (NEB). Copyright © by the Delegates of the Oxford University Press and the Syndics of the Cambridge University Press, 1961, 1970. Reprinted by permission.

New King James Version (NKJV). Copyright © 1979, 1980, 1982 Thomas Nelson, Inc. Used by permission.

New Revised Standard Version (NRSV) of the Bible, copyright 1989 by the Division of Christian Education of the National Council of the Churches of Christ in the USA. Used by permission. All rights reserved.

The Living Bible (TLB), © 1971. Used by permission of Tyndale House Publishers, Inc., Wheaton, IL 60189. All rights reserved.

Scriptures marked KJV are from the King James Version.

Library of Congress Cataloging-in-Publication Data

Galloway, Dale E.
    On-purpose leadership : multiplying your ministry by becoming a leader of leaders / by Dale E. Galloway ; with Warren Bird.
        p. cm.
    Includes bibliographical references.
    ISBN 0-8341-1882-3
        1. Christian leadership. I. Bird, Warren. II. Title.

    BV652.1 .G35 2000
    253—dc21

                                                                    00-066751

CONTENTS

16 80

115056

Introduction

If you're not a growing person yourself, your church cannot go to new places. Anytime you're thrown into a church that's beyond where you've grown, you won't be able to handle it. My passion is to help you keep growing in order to become a maximum-impact leader. I want to help you achieve the breakthroughs you need for both you *and* the church you serve to go forward.

Our starting point is Jesus.

Jesus is the greatest leader who ever lived. His public ministry of three years has become the cornerstone of human history. Even a secular magazine like *Time* affirms: "It would require much exotic calculation to deny that the single most powerful figure—not merely in these two millenniums but in all human history—has been Jesus of Nazareth." Why? Because, the cover article continues, "a serious argument can be made that no one else's life has proved remotely as powerful and enduring as that of Jesus" (Price 1999). Jesus' influence was exemplary by any standard used: His integrity of character, what He did, what lasting results have remained, and how He entrusted His leadership through others.

You can't look at Jesus' life without sensing that everything He did was with a purpose. He did nothing without purpose. Even His leaving had purpose.

Consider this sampling of Jesus' sense of purpose:

- Jesus knew His life on earth was part of a larger purpose: "For even the Son of Man did not come to be served, but to serve, and to give his life as a ransom for many" (Mark 10:45).
- Jesus' itinerate ministry had purpose: "For the Son of Man came to seek and to save what was lost" (Luke 19:10).
- Jesus knew that purpose would have a profound impact on others: "I have come that they may have life, and have it to the full" (John 10:10). "I am the bread of life. He who comes to me will never go hungry, and he who believes in me will never be thirsty" (6:35).
- Jesus did not allow himself to be diverted from that purpose: "But he said, 'I must preach the good news of the kingdom of God to the other towns also, because that is why I was sent'" (Luke 4:43).
- Jesus' day-to-day ministry was guided by that purpose: "As the time approached for him to be taken up to heaven, Jesus resolutely set out for Jerusalem" (9:51).
- Jesus knew He had been sent from heaven: "I came from God and now am here. I have not come on my own; but he sent me" (John 8:42).
- Jesus also knew that His early life would be directed toward the Cross: "From that time on Jesus began to explain to his disciples that he must go to Jerusalem and suffer many things at the hands of the elders, chief

priests and teachers of the law, and that he must be killed and on the third day be raised to life" (Matt. 16:21).

- Jesus' "I am" claims show that His purpose was linked to who He is: "I am the way and the truth and the life. No one comes to the Father except through me" (John 14:6). "I am the vine; you are the branches. If a man remains in me and I in him, he will bear much fruit; apart from me you can do nothing" (15:5).

- Jesus not only taught His disciples but also showed them how to lead. He told them, "I have set you an example that you should do as I have done for you" (John 13:15).

Jesus' purpose required men and women to be trained as leaders. Robert Coleman's classic book *The Master Plan of Evangelism* emphasizes that Jesus spent three-fourths of His ministry training the Twelve. Jesus' "concern was not with programs to reach the multitudes, but with men whom the multitudes would follow . . . Men were to be his method of winning the world to God" (21).

During that training, Jesus turned disciples into apostles, and followers into leaders. Jesus' model of leadership brought out the best in those who followed Him. Their watchwords, as they passed Jesus' baton to still others, were some of the most dangerous words recorded in the New Testament: "Follow my example, as I follow the example of Christ" (1 Cor. 11:1).

If you want to bring out the best in others, as Jesus did, you have to lead with an awareness of your purpose, just as Jesus did. You must know what your mission is, what your core values are, where you are, and where God is calling you to be.

You must learn how to get beyond yourself. Ninety percent of pastors never get beyond their own reach; they don't know how to pass the leader-making mantle to people who, in turn, pass it on to others. Otherwise your ministry influence will not extend beyond a single cell.

How do you get beyond your reach? You might be standing in your own way! You might be the cork in the bottle! The message of this book is that the problem might be with you, not your circumstances. At the same time, this book will show you a new perspective that will enable you to grow in how you think and how you use your time. It will enable you to lead other people with a purpose and get handles on the breakthrough points you need to reach new levels.

It's not enough simply to be called a leader; you must have a sense of purposefulness as well. The world is dotted with churches that have been taken to one level but can't go any farther because the leadership didn't know how to go forward or perhaps wasn't willing to do so.

The key to doing extraordinary ministry through others stems from learning to influence the influencers. This book will help you as a church leader break free from where you are now in order to move to the next level. Many people learn how to work through others leaders. However, a strategic leap occurs when you learn how to help those lay leaders develop *additional* leaders. This three-level perspective—making disciples who make disciples—represents a whole new skill set. Yet this model comes from our Lord himself, both in His teaching (Matt.

28:19-20) and in His example. Likewise it was what the apostles modeled and taught (see 2 Tim. 2:2).

How do you move from their present leadership style to a more purposeful and strategic approach? This book will show you how to become a visionary who is ever reaching into the future while also being realistic about where you are now.

One of the great gifts to this generation is my friend Rick Warren's book *The Purpose-Driven Church.* It made many churches think through what they are doing as a church. I want to help leaders ask the same question of their ministry and leadership, and learn how to carry it out in the most effective way. As business leader Peter Drucker reminds us in *The Effective Executive,* there's a world of difference between someone who does things right and someone else who does the right things. I want to help you do the right things.

In 1972 my wife, Margi, and I started New Hope Community Church in a drive-in theater in Portland, Oregon. Through the years God used us to develop ministries to address the needs of thousands of unchurched people. In 1995, when I accepted the call to become dean of the Beeson Institute, New Hope Community had 6,400 members.

Several times in this book you will hear about various experiences from New Hope and from prior pastorates as illustrations of the principles of leadership I propose. I express praise to God for all He did. The believers who found new life in Christ are trophies of His grace! I endeavored to serve as an instrument in His hands.

If Jesus set our model of *On-Purpose Leadership,* then what exactly is *your* purpose? What is your development process for getting there and for taking others with you? I invite you to reach new levels as a leader as you read the following pages.

SECTION ONE

Break Free from the Status Quo

1

WHAT IS YOUR PASSION?

One of the watchwords in today's church is *vision*. Pastors preach on it. Boards discuss it. Authors write on it. Seminaries teach about it. Conferences focus on it. These days a person can't hang around pastors and church leaders long without talking about vision.

Vision is seeing what is not yet here—visualizing something before it is. Researcher George Barna says, "Vision for ministry is a clear mental image of a preferable future imparted by God to His chosen servants and is based upon an accurate understanding of God, self, and circumstances" (1992, 28).

I find it odd how often people describe their dreams for the future, and yet the picture they paint has nothing to do with their passion, giftedness, or life experiences. Passion is also an outworking of a person's spiritual giftedness, life preparation, and life experiences. Vision won't contradict any of these direction shapers. We serve a God who brings order to His Church, not confusion (see 1 Cor. 14:40).

If our vision comes from God, we will also have a passion for it. In fact, passion fuels vision. If we don't have the emotional fire and heartfelt enthusiasm known as passion, we won't have true vision. Lon Solomon, who pastors McLean Bible Church just outside Washington, D.C., identifies that same sequence in the church's 10-year growth from 250 to 7,000, "I didn't really have a vision, but I had a passion. I have a passion for reaching secular people because I was a secular person. . . . I asked, 'How can my church reach "me"'?" [2000, "Fix Your Gaze," 24].

Passion fuels vision.

Passion shows itself in different ways in different people. In every great, cutting-edge church that I have observed, I have found this common thread: a passion to reach the lost for Christ. If you don't have passion to share the gospel with those who need it, you won't have vision that matches God's heart.

If you struggle with identifying a clear and compelling vision for your ministry, then look to your spiritually shaped passions for clues.

How to Cultivate, Refuel, and Increase Passion

Would you like to cultivate a greater spiritual passion? If you or I want long-term staying power in ministry, we need to identify ways to refuel and increase our passion by the power of the Holy Spirit. God will supply the motivating passion we need in the following ways:

1. **Passion often comes out of where a person met God and where he or she has been touched spiritually.** People who found Christ through New Hope Community Church, the church my wife, Margi, and I started, when it met in an outdoor, drive-in movie theater tended to have a passion for helping the drive-in ministry succeed. Someone who came to Christ in a small group often shows a passion for small groups. People who met God in other places have a passion for those other ministries.

2. **Ongoing passion also comes from quiet times with God.** As you walk with God, do you continually ask yourself, "What would Jesus do in this situation?" or "How would Jesus feel now?" Are you passionate about what Jesus is passionate about? What breaks Jesus' heart likewise should break your heart and mine. The more times of oneness we have with God, the greater our passion will be.

3. **Passion also comes from spending time with others who are passionate.** They're contagious! I have a videotape from Bill Hybels on his vision for Willow Creek Community Church. He shares his unashamed passion for evangelism, the "fire that burns in [his] bones" (Jer. 20:9, TLB) for seeing every unchurched Harry and Mary in metro Chicago come to Christ and become fully devoted followers. I can't watch that video without having my passion rekindled.

4. **Another way to renew passion is by taking time away to dream.** A vacation is sometimes needed to stoke passion. Attending a conference can be an investment in renewal. For many years Margi and I journeyed to the Robert H. Schuller Institute for Successful Church Leadership. Often we brought along a group of leaders from the church. There at the Crystal Cathedral we heard pacesetters who had dared to dream a great dream for the glory of God through the expansion of His kingdom. These gifted communicators inspired their hearers to think big. We left invigorated with the greatness of God and renewed in our passion to be difference-makers. Like Abraham when told to count the stars (Gen. 15:5-6), our sights were lifted to new heights, beyond our ability to imagine or think. We inevitably caught their God-instilled passion for how to reach lost people.

What About Adversity?

Adversity refines passion. I don't know if a Christian can have passion without some suffering. There's no gain without some pain. I've never seen anybody take a church to the next level of ministry without paying a price.

One of the core ideas in my book *Dare to Discipline Yourself* is this: You have to deny lesser things to gain greater things.

Also, nothing quenches passion as quickly as sin. I remember a friend confronting me about my response to a painful disappointment in my life. "Dale, you're bitter," he said frankly. He was right. I had allowed a lack of forgiveness to dim and color my passion for the things of God.

I needed to learn that surrender to the Lordship of Jesus included not only my will but also my pain, ill feelings, rights, and whatever else would steal passion from what God had called me to do. A focused passion is impossible to maintain without a sense of surrender to the Holy Spirit. There is no mission without surrender. For some people, such as E. Stanley Jones, the best biblical term for this kind of surrender is *sanctification*.

Finally, in the surrendered life, we are willing to make whatever changes are needed along the way, both in ourselves and in the churches we lead. I heard Bill Hybels speak about endurance in ministry, explaining that leaders sometimes must make painful changes in order to have long endurance. For example, suppose a staff person who has been with me a long time needs to move on. The change will be painful. However, if I don't make the change, the situation will drag me down and keep me from enduring.

Saddleback and Willow Creek as Examples

Is there a scriptural and practical foundation for this idea of passion? Rick Warren, founding pastor of Saddleback Community Church, which has one of the largest worship attendances in America, calls it "heart." He's referring to whatever we love to do.

"For out of the overflow of the heart the mouth speaks" (Matt. 12:34).

"Above all else, guard your heart, for it is the wellspring of life" (Prov. 4:23).

"Delight yourself in the LORD and he will give you the desires of your heart" (Ps. 37:4).

Others who emphasize the idea of passion include the team of Willow Creek pastors who created the ministry mobilization tool known as *Network*. They draw from the motivations of people like the apostle Paul:

"But when God, who set me apart from birth and called me by his grace, was pleased to reveal his Son in me so that I might preach him among the Gentiles, I did not consult any man" (Gal. 1:15-16).

"It has always been my ambition to preach the gospel where Christ was not known" (Rom. 15:20).

Both of these great congregations have built the concept of passion into their training curriculum. Passion, according to authors Bruce Bugbee, Don Cousins, and Bill Hybels in the *Network Participant's Guide*, answers the "where you're moti-

Passion Destroyers

Any of the following actions or attitudes can keep you from having the passion that God wants to stir in your heart.

Bitterness
Disobedience
Distraction
Ego trips
Lack of focus
Physical fatigue
Selfish greed
Unwillingness to
    make painful
    changes

vated to serve" question. Participants at Willow Creek learn that "passion is the God-given desire that compels us to make a difference in a particular ministry . . . When you have a passion for an area of ministry, you are more enthusiastic and motivated to serve" (1994, 14-15).

Rick Warren uses the acronym S.H.A.P.E. to describe Saddleback Church's ministry discovery and placement process. When asked, "How has God shaped me for ministry?" the church helps its people identify Spiritual Gifts, Heart, Abilities, Personality, and Experience.

From there a person goes through an interview process with the help of a lay ministry guide. The purpose is to identify three or four possible ministry settings. Then the individual meets with the staff members who supervise the ministries being considered. Finally the person begins the ministry and also attends monthly meetings called S.A.L.T. (Saints And Leaders Training), a two-hour training rally designed for core members of the church.

These churches, and many others, understand the crucial linkage of vital passion to effective vision.

Passion Is the "Heart" of the Matter

In a Leadership Network forum, where Peter Drucker and Lyle Schaller served as principal resources, Schaller summarized his view on the need for passion in ministry today: "The critical issue in society is a shortage of competent leadership with the kind of *passion* that generates followers. This is also *the* critical issue for churches. What in your congregation are *you* doing to produce leaders for the next generation?"

> **Ways to Test a Passion or Vision to See If It's from God:**
> 1. Would this be a great thing for God?
> 2. Would it help hurting people?
> 3. Would it bring the best out in me?
> 4. Is it something God has given me to do?

(NetFax No. 86, 12/8/97, italics added).

The sooner you and I can identify, cultivate, and increase a passion for things that matter to God, the more He will unleash in each of us a clear vision for the future. At New Hope Community Church we often spoke of the desperate need to reach the unchurched thousands in greater Portland. When my passion behind those words was compelling, that's when God seemed to use us to make the greatest impact. Nothing is more powerful than the synergy created when God's people led by a Spirit-filled leader come together with passion.

2

YOUR VISION WILL GIVE YOU YOUR MAP

Tell me your dream and I'll tell you your future. There's nothing like a dream to give you a map to follow. Acts 16 tells the story of how Paul "had a vision of a man of Macedonia standing and begging him, 'Come over to Macedonia and help us'" (v. 9). Eugene Peterson's *The Message* titles that chapter "A Dream Gave Paul His Map."

My favorite subject is vision. I love to talk of dreaming great dreams for Christ and the Kingdom. If I had to choose one gift for pastors and church leaders, it would be the ability to see God's specific dream for their place of ministry. This chapter will help you learn how to find and follow God's "map" for your church's future.

Seek It

Nothing momentous happens in a church until a man or woman opens up to receive God's vision or dream. His dream makes you jump out of bed. The excitement wakes you up at night. It stretches you beyond where you are, taking you to new places of faith.

When you are possessed by a great vision, people rally to it. They believe God for great things.

Heb. 11 recaps the stories of men and women who believed God for the impossible. They saw something before it was physically in sight. They allowed God to work through their lives. They led others to cooperate with God to bring into existence what was not yet here. One of the Bible's best pictures of vision is captured at the beginning of that chapter: "Now faith is being sure of what we hope for and certain of what we do not see. This is what the ancients were commended for" (vv. 1-2).

How far do you see beyond the people you're leading? Vision is foresight with insight. Vision transforms and transcends. Vision sees where God sees— where God wants to take you and your ministry. The Holy Spirit, as God's agent of communication, brings vision and dreams to people, according to the story of Pentecost in Acts 2.

Do you want the Holy Spirit to communicate a vision into your spirit? Then get away on a spiritual retreat, perhaps with other friends or fellow leaders. Armed with Bible and devotional reading, get on your knees, call out to God, and wait. Seek God in prayer and in the Word until the Holy Spirit comes into your inner spirit to show you God's will, vision, and dream for His church.

Summarize It

Can you summarize your vision in one sentence or in one word picture? George Barna says, "For vision to become effective it must be simple enough to be remembered and be specific enough to give direction" (*The Power of Vision*, 138)

When I planted New Hope Community Church, our big, hairy, holy, audacious goal was "to reach the unchurched thousands in Portland, Oregon." In 1972, with no people and no money, Margi and I had that vision and began to reach toward it. Some people laughed, but not because they didn't understand — they laughed because they thought it was ridiculous or impossible to be achieved.

God-given vision takes a church forward.

Too many people say they have vision, but they can't put it into words. Calvin Miller quips, "A lightning bug lives most confused. He hasn't any mind and he wanders through existence with his headlights on behind." God-given vision takes a church forward. It accomplishes the great task to which God has called it. If you can't specify what that task is, then maybe you don't have vision yet.

Sell It

Leadership begins with vision. When people buy into your vision, they buy into your leadership. The first job of the leader is to cast vision — to help people see the potential before them.

The story of Nehemiah illustrates this process. "Then I said to them, 'You see the trouble we are in: Jerusalem lies in ruins, and its gates have been burned with fire. Come, let us rebuild the wall of Jerusalem, and we will no longer be in disgrace.' I also told them about the gracious hand of my God upon me and what the king had said to me. They replied, 'Let us start rebuilding.' So they began this good work" (Neh. 2:17-18).

Sloganize It

Perhaps the best way to communicate your dream to your congregation is through slogans. You can barely find a page in *The Purpose-Driven Church* that doesn't contain one of Rick's short, memorable sayings. He tells his congregation that he sits in his study, working hard to devise catchy slogans because he is convinced they are effective communication tools.

Other churches use slogans with similar results. Some of the slogans we used at New Hope to describe our dream for lay ministry included: "Do something great for God," "Make your life count," "Make the most of the life you have," "Everyone a minister," and "Join the team."

Rick Warren also mentions other ways to instill vision:

1. **Scriptures.** Preach the vision each time you teach from the Bible.

2. **Symbols.** From artwork to architecture, you communicate through the visual messages you associate with your church.

3. **Stories.** In the beginning, you build people's faith by talking about what God will do in the future through them. Soon enough you can begin to brag on what God has done, and the momentum will continue to grow around the vision.

4. **Specific Applications.** Vision doesn't connect with people until it shows them, "How do I participate?" Most successful church-facility expansions, for example, don't focus on the six- and seven-digit numbers needed. Instead, they offer a specific application: "You may buy one seat for an unchurched person by giving $5 a week for three years." Many people buy multiple seats, because they can understand it so clearly.

5. **Spending Time with the Influencers.** Nothing persuades more than face-to-face interactions as you share your heart with others.

Stretch Toward It

When we decided to start the church in Portland, I made a list of 10 possible places, and I went to each of them. Only one said yes—a drive-in theater—and that became our humble beginning. As soon as Margi and I got one small group going, I began to promise our small drive-in congregation, "Someday we're going to have hundreds of small groups all over this city, led by dedicated people. Someday we'll have all kinds of need-meeting ministries that help people come into fellowship with Christ." Over and over, I went out on a limb of faith, at one time even mortgaging our home to come up with needed "seed" moneys.

At each point, I had to dare to risk failure to gain success. Looking back on my pastoral ministry of 32 years at four different churches, I never reached a level where I had not been before without stretching and risking.

When I get to heaven, I'll say, "Jesus, I love You—but why did You almost let me drown so many times before You came and, like the winds of the great Exodus, parted the sea to provide the next step?" I think I'll hear, "If I had done it sooner, you'd tell people how great *you* are. I wanted you to depend on *Me* and give *Me* the glory."

These exciting opportunities don't happen unless I'm willing to stretch, to risk everything to achieve the goals for Christ and His kingdom. When that happens, God gets the glory.

Stick with It

When setbacks come—and they will—stay with the vision. When people don't get it, try again. When obstacles rise up, remember that anything worthwhile will encounter opposition. Usually the more worthwhile, the more hurtles you will need to cross.

See the problems not as stop signs but as road signs along the road to fulfilling the vision. Remember that it's always darkest before the morning.

In order to get along well with people, you need to be flexible. That involves giving up lots of things. But don't give up the vision. Stick with the stuff. As Paul counseled, "Therefore, my dear brothers, stand firm. Let nothing move you. Always give yourselves fully to the work of the Lord, because you know that your labor in the Lord is not in vain" (1 Cor. 15:58).

Whenever I am discouraged and tempted to give up the dream, I always remember how Jesus stuck with the Father's vision for His work: "Jesus resolutely set out for Jerusalem" (Luke 9:51).

What are you willing to die for? A great vision from God is worth giving everything. It enables you to make your one life count for the most it can.

Can you identify that kind of vision in your own life? If so, you couldn't ask for any better gift from God.

Are You Using These Opportunities to Spread Vision to Your Church?

1. **Preaching.** As you apply God's Word to life today, how are you leading people on a journey toward a dream you share together? One of the ways to lead people into a vision is to preach it.
2. **Monthly Publication.** Do you distribute a regular newsletter, fax, or E-mail to your congregation? If so, you can use the front-page article to cast vision.
3. **Sunday Bulletin.** What image do you want the worship guide to convey? Use the look and content to communicate what you believe the people need to hear.
4. **Staff Meeting.** In most cases, the senior pastor should set the agenda, flow, and mood of your ongoing staff training.
5. **Staff Selection.** If you don't have authority to hire and fire staff, learn to work through the appropriate committee in order to maximize your influence.
6. **Church Board.** Spend a lot of time with whoever chairs the board or shapes the agenda. In most cases it is very appropriate for you to have a significant say.
7. **Other Opinion Leaders.** Make time to build consensus with various opinion leaders. Never go into a board meeting unprepared and unaware of what you think the outcome will be.
8. **Other Visionaries.** Hang out with other visionaries in your congregation, and encourage them to help spread the vision.
9. **Worship Arts.** You can cast vision by catchphrases, by stories, by testimonies, by dramatizing of certain needs, and by celebrating major victories. When you cheer something in public, you are saying, "This is very important to what we're about."

3

Does Your Heart Beat with the Heartbeat of God?

Lost people matter to God. Do they matter to you? Do they matter in your church? Do they matter enough to make this concept your congregation's primary core value?

Do you want to draw people to your church who haven't yet been reached for Christ? This passion is at the heart of every church that is effective in reaching unchurched people.

In mid-September 1999 I took a group of Beeson pastors to Ohio to visit Grove City Church of the Nazarene. I had pioneered and planted that congregation in 1963. In the worship service we visited, Senior Pastor Bob Huffaker cast the vision to see 100 people baptized in six weeks, which would be the last Sunday of October. Dr. Huffaker modeled what business author Jim Collins calls a BHAG (pronounced *bee*-hag)—a Big, Hairy, Audacious Goal.

I thought to myself, *This guy is really out on the limb.* But as someone has said, "Out on the limb is where the fruit is."

On October 31 I could not resist driving three hours to this suburb of Columbus. I couldn't wait to see what happened.

What a celebration took place as we witnessed the baptisms and testimonies of 137 new converts that morning. The church even had to rent an extra baptistery for the occasion!

I later learned that the Sunday after Easter was another big baptism day. When the 27th and final person scheduled to be baptized came out of the water, someone from the congregation spontaneously asked if he, too, could be baptized as a sign of following Christ. No baptismal gowns were available, so he entered the water in his Sunday clothes. The moment was so moving that others followed suit. By the end of the morning, 85 people had been baptized!

Too Much Evangelistic Passion?

Do churches like Grove City put too much energy into evangelism? I don't think so, because lost people matter to God. But the more important question is: What do *you* think? How important is this core value to you? How important is it to your church?

The more I read the Bible, the more I see this value at the core of Scripture—running from Genesis to Revelation.

1. The mission of Jesus was to live and die on a cross so that sinners could be put in right relationship with God—"while we were still sinners, Christ died for us" (Rom. 5:8).

2. The central message of the Cross teaches that lost people matter to God. Jesus said He came "to seek and to save what was lost" (Luke 19:10).

3. The most important decision of eternity underscores this value: "For what will it profit them to gain the whole world and forfeit their life?" (Mark 8:36, NRSV).

4. The central mission of the church, found in the Great Commission and the Great Commandment, involves reaching out to lost people whom God loves.

5. The most central teaching of the church, reflected in John 3:16—perhaps the most-quoted verse in the entire New Testament—involves reaching lost people.

6. Taken a whole, the entire Bible is the history of God's salvation of lost people.

7. Perhaps the three greatest parables ever taught, presented in Luke 15, all underscore the same idea. According to verses 1-2, it was the religious crowd, the Pharisees, the keepers of the traditions, who were most disturbed at Jesus because He reached out to sinners. Jesus seized the opportunity to teach three parables in which the key word is *lost*: lost sheep, lost coin, lost son. In the third parable, which also goes by the name *prodigal son*, something takes place that never happened in the Jewish family: the father went out seeking, looking, searching for the lost son.

8. This core value is one that can be directly applied to every culture, every generation, and every country.

9. All ministry that has high impact in changing lives is relational. Few core values are more relational than a compelling sense that lost people matter to God.

10. This core value seems to be the heartbeat of God and the heartbeat of churches that are making a difference in impacting people. It's built into the soul of thousands of churches of every shape and size. It needs to be built into my soul as well.

Too Much Preaching on the Subject?

The phrase "lost people matter to God" has been burned into hearts across the world from the heart of Bill Hybels, who is the pastor of the largest-attended church in North America, Willow Creek Community Church, in a northwest suburb of Chicago. I heard Bill say that 12 to 18 of his sermons each year touch on this central core value.

Many would pick Bill Hybels out as being one of the outstanding leaders in the Church today, and I would agree. However, I personally think his greatest contribution to the Church is the way he passionately communicates that lost people matter to God. He emphasizes that if you don't keep this the primary focus above others, it will get lost.

Let me illustrate. A church that loses its emphasis on this value is like a company that stops selling. It can improve everything else it does, but if sales stop, the company will die. The company that says "We don't need a sales force anymore" will lose it all.

I've taken various Beeson pastor groups to Willow Creek's Church Leadership Conference almost a dozen times. Every time I go, Bill Hybels holds high a torch under this core value—lost people matter to God. As Bill pours out the passion of his soul for the lost, it always connects with my spirit to do everything I can to reach unchurched people.

A Mistake Willow Creek Almost Made

One of the videotapes I show my Beeson pastor class each year is Bill Hybels' message on vision-casting. Shortly after Willow Creek's 20th anniversary celebration, Bill cast a new five-year vision to the congregation. One part of that vision was to grow in weekend attendance from 15,000 to 20,000.

At the halfway mark through the five-year run, they were halfway there with 17,500 in weekly attendance. What a difference a passionate vision for the lost makes! As John Maxwell says, "Our priorities determine our effectiveness as leaders."

At that time Bill Hybels commented that when he started the five-year run, he had made the decision that his resources, energies, and attention would divide equally among each of the five components of what he thought made up the foundation of a biblically functioning church. He gave 20 percent of his attention to each of the five Gs, as Willow calls them: *grace* (showing lost people that they matter to God and can experience salvation through Christ), *growth* (helping people go forward in their faith), *groups* (finding biblical community through a small group), *gifts* (finding and using your spiritual gifts), and *giving* (putting God first in our stewardship of resources).

Then he discovered that this ratio was a big mistake. It looked good on paper, but it didn't happen in practice. The first G needed not just 20 percent but more like 40 percent in order to keep it in focus and on target.

According to Hybels, the "grace" core value requires more emphasis than the others for two reasons. First, Satan attacks a church in this area to try to stop its outreach. Second, people being who they are tend to move away from reaching out. Instead they become settlers.

He's right. Good people will begin to make a case for more discipling, which sounds very biblical, but it can be an escape or an excuse from doing the work of reaching the lost. In the making of a disciple, evangelism and growth go hand in hand.

A Mistake We, Too, Want to Avoid

Looking back in my own life in churches I've served, I noticed that among the core values, if I didn't keep the torch lit under the theme that lost people matter to God, it began to fade.

I have studied the leadership patterns of the senior pastor in the cutting-edge churches I have visited. These leaders have different styles and gifts, but there are certain common threads that run through all of them. Virtually all have visionary and people skills, the ability to influence the influencers, the big picture perspective, and a stick-to-it quality that perseveres in spite of obstacles or setbacks.

But the most predominant characteristic I see in churches making a difference is an inner passion for the lost. They believe in their heart of hearts that lost people matter to God. As George Hunter, Asbury Seminary professor and author of *Church for the Unchurched*, says, "The Great Commission has to be something like a Magnificent Obsession."

Practical Ideas for Staying Focused

How is your heart? Does it beat with the heartbeat of God? The answer involves more than asking yourself, "How many engagements or lunches have I had with the unchurched in the last 30 days?" or "How many sermons or teachings on this have I given?"

Without intentionally and repeatedly focusing your church on this core value, your people will drift from it. They'll simply become "comfortable." Here are 10 effective ways to help keep your church focused on this primary core value:

1. **Vision.** Their vision is fueled by passion for the lost.

2. **Core Value.** Their written core values explicitly state: "Lost people matter to God."

3. **Preach.** Their preaching visits this core value 15 to 20 times a year.

4. **Training.** Their equipping materials, such as Willow's *Contagious Christianity* or Steve Sjogren's *Servant Evangelism*, reinforce this core value. They provide different kinds of training for different people, depending on where their gifts and comfort zones are.

5. **Mission Trips.** They offer short-term missions trips that get people so centered in reaching lost people that they, like my daughter when she returned from Africa, eagerly witness about their faith to all their friends.

6. **Special Emphases.** They give high visibility to commitment points such as baptisms. They use those occasions to make a high impact on the need to reach the lost. When Lee Strobel was a teaching pastor at Willow Creek, in a sermon two months before Easter, he challenged everyone to pick one person who needed to be won to Christ and to pray for that person at 1:00 each afternoon. Imagine the spiritual power centered on those after-lunch prayers!

7. **Testimonies.** They feature testimonies of those who have crossed from

darkness into light. This raises people's awareness of their relationships and teaches them about evangelism.

8. **Bridge Events.** They design bridge-building events, such as a hunting breakfast of 800 to 900 men that I attended, which included a compelling presentation of the gospel.

9. **Goal Setting.** They set goals, such as the Grove City Church of the Nazarene example earlier in this chapter.

10. **Need-Meeting Ministries.** They create need-meeting ministries, such as New Hope Community Church's support and recovery groups, which reached thousands of people during my years there as pastor. Year after year we demonstrated that the more need-meeting ministries you have, the more people you will reach. (Can you name your need-meeting ministries?)

You Can Find a Way

My life story reflects several different strategies of evangelism. For example, I grew up in a revival tradition. So as a young pastor, I emphasized altar calls as a paradigm for how people came to Christ.

Then in 1963, when I started the new church in Grove City, Ohio, I went door to door, praying that God would help me know how to talk to people. Six months later I met a Campus Crusade for Christ leader at Ohio State University. Over lunch, he taught me the Four Spiritual Laws, scratching them out on a napkin. Thanks to this tool, my door-to-door encounters noticeably increased in their fruitfulness. Last year I was a guest at that church, and I met 20 to 25 people I had led to Christ in the '60s.

In 1972, Margi and I launched New Hope Community Church in Portland, Oregon. During that era, on one of my visits to the Robert H. Schuller Institute for Successful Church Leadership, I learned how he used a pastor's welcome class to lead people to Christ. I instituted a similar five-week class in Portland and saw people commit themselves to Christ—thousands as the years went by.

From David Yonggi Cho and others I discovered the power of friendship evangelism through small groups. Now the impact of evangelism was multiplied even further as several hundred Tender Loving Care groups met every week, each with an evangelistic component.

Each of these evangelism paradigms released me to lead my people into reaching more people in the harvest than before. I believe it was the Holy Spirit at work, using the desire of my heart to bring about these evangelistic breakthroughs.

The same experience can be true for you. The concept that lost people matter to God must be built into the very center of your church if you're going to reach people. If this is your primary value, you will find a strategy for reaching out to lost people, no matter how difficult a context you might face.

I once read a quote by C. T. Mott, an evangelist 100 years ago: "If Jesus Christ be God, and died for me, then no sacrifice can be too great for me to make for him." If your heartbeat is God's heartbeat for the lost, then with God's Holy Spirit directing, you, too, will find a way.

4

THE FRUIT OF A HIGH-IMPACT CHURCH

How is the church you serve changing? Is it becoming more alive? Is it out-ward-focused, serious about Christ's commandment to make disciples of all nations (Matt. 28:19-20)?

If you are leading a vibrant, healthy church, there's a good chance it will soon become a larger congregation. As your fellowship meets people's needs in Jesus' name, and it experiences the joys of changed lives and new births in Christ, your church can have a spillover effect to impact the entire Christian community around you in positive ways.

Smaller churches can be wonderful. They can provide many benefits. For example, my father was a pastor and district superintendent. He and a half dozen fellow pastors all came from the same small rural church in Arkansas. As Lyle Schaller's book *The Small Membership Church: Scenarios for Tomorrow* affirms: "I predict a viable future for the congregation of 100 or fewer" (1995, 12). The small church is not about to disappear.

However, one of the most significant ecclesiastical changes of the 20th century was the emergence of the large regional church. Today half of the churchgoers on a typical weekend in North America can be found in the largest 13 percent of churches, according to Schaller. He also predicts that by 2025, half of churchgoing Protestants will be found in only 10 percent of churches. By 2050, only 7 percent of churches will account for one-half of all Protestant worshipers, he projects (*Net Results* 10/97, 10; *Net Results* 7/96, 27).

In spending my lifetime growing churches to become larger churches, I've watched the lift that a budding church can give to a whole community. If they maintain a strong evangelistic pulse, highly visible churches can bless and bene-fit the greater community and surrounding Christian bodies in the following ways:

1. **They reach people other churches can't reach.** Certain people are at-tracted to things that seem successful and growing. For example, the CEO of a large company will in most cases not think about going to a small church. Big-

thinking people don't want to go to a smaller church unless it has a big vision, which often means it is in the process of growing larger.

2. **They reach people at different stages of need.** Typically, the larger the church, the more types of groups it can sponsor. Someone whose father is dying of Alzheimer's disease can find great help in a church-sponsored support group of others facing the same circumstances. Groups such as Operation Desert Storm vets and Christian Businesswomen's Club can draw many people who might not otherwise be reached. At New Hope we had 200 need-meeting ministries reaching people from drug addicts to single moms. This scope of ministry is simply not possible for a smaller church.

3. **They offer multiple points of entry.** John Hurston's book *Caught in the Web* tells the story of the fastest-growing church in the history of Christendom, Yoido Full Gospel Church in Seoul, Korea, pastored by David Yonggi Cho. The image in Hurston's title refers not to one hook in the water, but rather to a large net. I have found that if prospects or newcomers are touched from five or six directions at once, rather than just from one angle, they're more likely to respond. People usually need to see or hear something many times before it sinks in.

4. **They multiply the touches people receive.** Once people do visit the church, they must find a place where they fit or else they'll drop out. In a little church, you have one or two ways people can connect. There may be a choir, a women's ministry, a youth program, and Sunday School or home groups. In many cases, that's it. The bigger the church, however, the more varied the opportunities to attract someone. When one thing doesn't reach or connect, another will.

5. **They provide stability when a family splits up.** At New Hope Community Church, I saw more than once how parents, though divorcing, both stayed at the church. Thanks to the church's size, they could attend different services, thereby not having to be with their former spouse, while allowing the children to be there every week.

6. **They tend to develop high-impact worship and marketplace preaching that hits people where they are and motivates them toward God.** Such churches are high on celebration, and they keep improving their worship to be even more attractive. As such, larger churches can provide a high quality of music, enabling them to meet the needs of those looking for musical excellence in ways smaller churches often don't have resources to offer. Talent attracts talent, both as participants in the musical programming and in the experiencing of it.

7. **They present a place of service for staff not particularly gifted to lead a single-pastorate church.** Some people are fantastic in a supportive, associate pastor's role. Others are not successful preachers, but they are great at administration or counseling. Still others have specialized gifts, such as ministry to down-and-outers or in other contexts that require the support of a larger church.

8. **They provide a broad range of opportunities for people to discover and use their spiritual gifts in ministry.** The bigger the church, the more variety in type and range of ministry. From teaching gifts to mercy gifts, the bigger the

church the more diversity is possible in most cases. Bigger churches are also more likely to represent more types of people across the social scale.

9. **They can sponsor ministry seven days a week.** For example, a large church can sponsor its own youth and children's camps so that it's not merely a one-week-of-the-year experience, but an ongoing experience in developing a child or youth in community. When I was a teenager I went to a district camp of 100 kids, drawn from a total of 140 churches. Then we returned home, not to see each other for another year. What a contrast from the one-church group that returns from camp and can continue to grow together week after week. New Hope Community Church would have 200 at our own youth camp, more than my entire district could muster each summer during my childhood.

10. **They have the ability to spend more resources on attracting and reaching lost people.** In a smaller church, salaries comprise 60 to 80 percent of the budget. Facility rent or mortgage tends to consume much of what remains. In a larger church, salaries represent about 50 percent of the budget, creating a larger pool of "discretionary" money. And a wise church designates at least 5 percent of its budget to local outreach.

11. **They can make a noticeable contribution to world evangelization.** A large church can quickly accomplish a big missions project. It can purchase Bibles for an entire town. It can send several teams to rebuild a community or church facility wiped out by a hurricane. It can support a missionary family, an entire Bible-translation project, or a church planting effort.

12. **They have the potential for becoming teaching centers.** In the early 1970s I went to Los Angeles to attend the newly launched Robert H. Schuller Institute for Successful Church Leadership. Five years later at New Hope Community Church, we began holding our own Church Growth Institute. Today several dozen major teaching-center churches exist all over the country. The benefits have included the breaking down of denominational walls. Loren Mead's book *The Once and Future Church* says that one of the major shifts taking place in the church today is the move from teaching seminaries to teaching congregations. A surprising number of large churches sponsor pastors' training schools, Bible colleges, or leadership training institutes. For several years, Bob Buford's Leadership Network and Leith Anderson's Wooddale Church sponsored a successful Teaching Church Network, where leaders in one church mentored leaders in another. Existing seminaries are developing more and more partnerships with large, thriving churches that function as teaching centers.

13. **They can make an impact on an entire section of a city.** Big projects can capture public attention and even headlines: "Who's the church that renovated the abandoned warehouse?" "You know the church that built a new facility along the freeway? I heard that it runs an after-school tutoring program for anyone in the community." An urban church in Metro New York did so much to beautify its decaying community that the mayor came to a worship service to express appreciation to the congregation. Because of our visibility in Portland, the city used New Hope's facilities for (and asked me to speak at) the high school baccalaureate services for five years in a row.

14. They provide a lift to all other churches on the surrounding ecclesiastical landscape. Researcher John Vaughan's books *The Large Church* and *Megachurches and America's Cities* point out that large churches tend to be located in geographic clusters near each other. If a town has one megachurch, it will likely soon grow up several. Why? I believe the reason is that larger churches can have a positive influence on surrounding churches. In Portland, members from churches of all shapes and sizes came to our annual 20/20 Vision conferences. Whenever we'd try something new—such as a telecare ministry or an improvement on our Tender Loving Care groups—10 years later 100 churches would be doing what we taught them.

It's not just site or size that makes a church great, but it's also the spirit.

It's not just site or size that makes a church great, but it's also spirit—the spirit of love and the Holy Spirit working in and through the people of the church.

I believe the next generation of leaders in North America will raise up the greatest churches in this continent's history. These large churches will have a unique opportunity to be centers of high impact not just for themselves, but for the greater Christian community as well. It's the kind of influence that benefits everyone.

5

MAKE THE MAIN THING THE MAIN THING

When I was a boy growing up in Columbus, Ohio, someone gave me a magnifying glass. In playing with it, I learned that by focusing it correctly, I could burn a hole in a piece of wood. If I merely waved it around, I wouldn't capture the sun's energy and get the results I wanted. Unless I focused it, I couldn't transform sunlight into firepower.

Have you discovered something similar about ministry? There is a power that comes from keeping proper focus on your ministry priorities. Today's church leaders have more advice available to them than any previous generation. "Do this," recommends one book. "Do that," explains a seminar. "Try this," suggests a magazine article. "Try that," counsels a friend.

With all the choices available today, if you scatter and scatter, you won't really accomplish anything. Here are six power points to help you focus on the main things and maintain power in your ministry:

POWER POINT 1:
Be selective in what you do.

Jesus attempted to do one thing: perform the work the Father gave Him to do. He said, "I tell you the truth, the Son can do nothing by himself; he can do only what he sees his Father doing, because whatever the Father does the Son also does" (John 5:19).

It's the narrow focus that gets the results. Jesus concentrated His priorities. He had a clear-cut goal: to seek and save the lost (see Luke 19:10). He set boundaries for himself. He didn't travel all over the Roman Empire. He knew His human limitations, so He spent two-thirds of His ministry time with the Twelve. Jesus' life maximized results by focusing time and energy on the few important things.

Jesus always hit the nail on the head with what He did. He became mighty by limiting himself.

No one person can do everything; no one should attempt everything. The leader who tries to do too many things is not going to accomplish anything. At age 15, I knew what college and seminary I would attend, and I had already dreamed of planting a congregation that would target the unchurched. This focus helped keep me on point.

Most pastors flounder if they try to do too many things. Many smaller churches try to take on far more than they're able to do.

What's the difference between a river and a swamp? Rivers move toward a destination while swamps go nowhere. A river has banks that limit it and take it to a destination. As a result, a river has focus and energy. People admire rivers, not swamps.

POWER POINT 2:
Make the main thing the main thing.

Do you ever find yourself majoring on majors or majoring on minors? It's amazing how many good opportunities come across a pastor's desk. But if you try to respond to too many of them, you'll end up like the swamp: going everywhere and nowhere.

I once had a staff member who was very capable but could not stay focused. By meeting together to talk regularly about the "main thing" for him, we kept his ministry on target, resulting in great success for him.

Real achievement comes by focusing on the right things and doing them over and over.

My older brother recently retired as senior vice president at a national insurance company. It took three new employees to replace all his responsibilities. When I asked him about this, he said he was very selective with his time; his priorities were always centered on the main things. He achieved success in building this great corporation by doing the right things year after year. He found the right stuff, and he stuck with it.

In pastoral ministry, there are no shortcuts to success. The tendency in today's age of instant coffee and overnight millionaires is to look primarily at the spectacular and the immediate. Instead, real achievement comes by focusing on the right things and doing them over and over.

What would you discover if you paused right now to make a list of all the things you do as a church leader? Giving consideration to what you do well, prayerfully pick out the three or four that are most important. Could these become your "main thing"?

By narrowing yourself to a handful of priorities for which you're gifted and can do well in your ministry setting, you will move toward getting better results. Then, as you begin to achieve greater results, you'll be able to use these "main things" as a foundation upon which to build other ministries.

If you're at a point where you are feeling overwhelmed, you may be trying to accomplish too many "main things." If you tackle too many things at once, you won't do any of them well. Be careful not to stretch yourself too thinly. You can't keep the main thing as the main thing if you're going too many directions at the same time.

POWER POINT 3:
Do "right things" more than "things rightly."

In *The Effective Executive* (1993), management expert Peter Drucker emphasizes the idea that managers do things the right way, but leaders do the right things. He explains that successful leaders are people who learn to pick out the right things and do them repeatedly until they see the fruit they desire.

Professional comedians practice a joke over and over until they get it right. I've heard it said that Jack Paar, predecessor of Johnny Carson and Jay Leno on NBC's *Tonight Show*, would experiment with a joke all day long. He'd try it on various audiences until it worked just the way he wanted. Similarly, if you can identify the "right thing" for you, that will become the focus of your ministry and calling. Do it over and over until you get a good result.

When storms come, these habits will work for you and will continue to bring harvest. At each low point in my personal life or ministry, I kept doing the right things even when the bottom fell out. God used the momentum to keep me going forward even as I struggled to regain overall balance.

At Portland's New Hope Community Church, I picked out the handful of activities that were the most important and fit my own gift mix and calling. For example, one of the things I majored on was small groups. They worked so well because they were a core value to me. I focused on creating leaders and apprentice-leaders for small groups, helping them develop prospect lists and providing training in how to lead an effective Tender Loving Care group.

I did this year after year. Eventually more than 500 groups were up and running. The congregation's phenomenal growth—from zero to more than 5,000 worshipers many Sundays—happened after many years of doing the right things.

POWER POINT 4:
Deny the lesser to gain the greater.

One reason I like to watch sports on television is to see my favorite players up close. When I watched the National Basketball Association's Michael Jordan, I saw the intensity and focus in his eyes. Those qualities explain why he won.

The same is true with coaches. I remember game 4 of the 1998 Eastern Divisional Championship between Indiana and Chicago. The score was very close. In the final minutes, each team kept edging the other by just a point or two. With $7/10$ of a second left in the game, Reggie Miller got the ball and shot a successful three-pointer, putting Indiana ahead. Most people assumed the game was over.

Then Michael Jordan grabbed the ball and tried a shot. As Jordan aimed and fired for the Bulls, the camera cut over to Indiana's Coach Larry Bird. He was stone-faced. He wasn't ready to celebrate. He was concentrated on Jordan.

The crowd's noise was intense, but real champions know how to focus out everything that is secondary. Jordan almost made a basket, which would have turned the game around. Both Jordan and Bird knew what was crucial in that final half-second, and they intuitively denied everything else in order to get there.

Success in ministry rarely occurs without an intentional denying of the lesser in order to gain the greater. This issue of self-denial is so important that I developed it in a book titled *Dare to Discipline Yourself.* It basically says that everyone needs two ingredients for success: self-discipline and focus.

POWER POINT 5:
Allow time between sowing and harvesting.

In seed planting, if you don't have the patience to wait, you won't ever see the acorn become a mighty oak. Mushrooms and squash grow quickly, but the towering oak takes time to reach its maturity. This principle is written into the core of nature.

So is the idea of sowing and reaping. As Scripture says, "Let us not become weary in doing good, for at the proper time we will reap a harvest if we do not give up" (Gal. 6:9).

Anything worthwhile takes time. The more worthwhile, the more focus and time is required.

Likewise, to build a great church simply takes time. As Scripture reminds us, "Be steadfast, immovable, always abounding in the work of the Lord" (1 Cor. 15:58, NASB). One of today's great enemies is instant gratification.

POWER POINT 6:
Let the Holy Spirit provide the power you need.

This point of focus is the most important. If your core "main thing" is for the Holy Spirit to work through your life, you will see greater things than you ever imagined. The power of God can move through you to make you more effective as you become a magnifier of Jesus.

We cannot do God's work effectively without the power of the Holy Spirit.

In ministry, your most fundamental power comes from getting lined up with the Holy Spirit and focusing on what God wants you to do. The "main things" God has for your life and ministry will fit your gifts and match your passion. They will fulfill the Great Commission and the Great Commandment. They will multiply you through other people. And you will look back and realize the success has come from supernatural origins, not from your wisdom nor from your strength alone.

The longer I serve the Lord, the more I realize the meaning of verses like Acts 1:8: "But you will receive power when the Holy Spirit comes on you." Nothing that endures can be built without the Holy Spirit.

We simply cannot do God's work effectively without the power of the Holy Spirit. How do you tap into that power? Many people have found clarity in an illustration I used in *20/20 Vision* (Galloway 1986, 48). I describe the major power lines that run along the edge of the New Hope Community Church property. They light up thousands of homes and one of Portland's hospitals. If you put a copper wire parallel to these overhead lines, you get a transfer of power.

The Holy Spirit is like those electrical cables. When we get our lines parallel to God's will for us, the power begins to be transferred into and through our lives. We become the magnifying glass through which God's power is focused.

This is exactly what God wants to happen. Jesus said, "I tell you the truth, anyone who has faith in me will do what I have been doing. He will do even greater things than these, because I am going to the Father" (John 14:12).

Focus on the main thing of the Holy Spirit in your life and ministry, and you will become an instrument for "greater things than these."

SECTION TWO

Break Free from Living as a "Lone Ranger"

6

INFLUENCING THE INFLUENCERS

An old grandfather puts his young grandson on the family donkey and begins the long journey to town. As they travel along the well-used pathway, passersby say, "Look at that selfish, spoiled kid riding the donkey while the old man is walking."

Not wanting people to criticize his grandson, the old man trades places with the boy.

Soon people begin to say, "Look at that lazy man making the child walk."

Not wanting to be called lazy, the grandfather gets off the donkey and walks alongside it.

Observers then begin to remark, "Look at those two stupid people walking when they could be riding the donkey."

Acting on their criticism, the grandfather seats both himself and his grandson on the donkey.

As they continue along, the next people watching them comment, "Look how they're brutalizing that donkey. They're going to break its back."

In response, they get off the donkey. They put the donkey on their backs, and carry it the rest of the way into town, arriving bedraggled, exhausted, and still the subject of bystander criticism.

The point of this fable is that if you try to please everyone, you, too, will quickly feel that you have a donkey on your back. Fortunately, being a people pleaser is not the ultimate goal of leadership.

Leadership goes far beyond making everyone happy. Instead, a leader learns how to influence other people for positive results. As your influence increases, so does your leadership.

A popular advertisement for E. F. Hutton says that when their company speaks, people listen. It implies that when a real leader speaks, people take note.

My friend John Maxwell says that leadership is all about that kind of influence. In fact, says Maxwell, "Leadership *is* influence, nothing more, and nothing less."

That's the opposite of what happened with this grandfather and his grandson.

God Calls Us to Be Influencers

God takes very seriously the way we manage our influence with others. Our credibility (who we are in relationship to someone) plus our communication (what we say) equals our influence. Influence comes from who you are and how you communicate that.

According to the following statements from Scripture, everyone has influence. Each of us has the privilege of using our influence for eternal good, to the glory of God:

- "You are the light of the world. . . . Let your light shine before men, that they may see your good deeds and praise your Father in heaven" (Matt. 5:14, 16).
- "Do not be overcome by evil, but overcome evil with good" (Rom. 12:21).
- "Make the most of your chances to tell others the Good News. Be wise in all your contacts with them" (Col. 4:5, TLB).

If I'm a good steward of what God has given me, then I must learn how to gain influence and use that influence to advance the kingdom of God. I want to influence people because this is what God has chosen and called me to do.

The issue of leadership goes to the heart of my motives. It asks whether I'm motivated by my ego or by the Holy Spirit.

Manipulation is influencing people for personal benefit, according to James Hunter's book *The Servant*, but the leadership model of Jesus is to influence people for mutual benefit—for their own well being, as well as for the good of others. Often you have to make a choice about how you will use your influence.

Influencing the Influencers

Effective leaders know what they are trying to accomplish, but they also know that they cannot lead people by directives. They have to use influence. In particular, they know that people of influence are their most valuable asset in influencing the rest of congregation to get there. They understand the power of influencing the influencer.

More important, they know that they need to build a leadership relationship with other leaders in the church body. They know that to influence the influencers they have to meet them where they are and then take them where they need to go.

Earning Real Influence

You can't buy influence, you can't force it, and you can't demand it. It has little to do with titles or educational degrees.

Instead, you must earn influence. I've found seven different ways to gain influence. Each comes when you are a leader characterized by:

1. **Clear Vision.** People will follow you only if they know where you're going. People follow a leader who gives clear direction.

2. **Credibility.** I once had a youth pastor who made great announcements of what he was going to do, but a week later he had forgotten his promises. Same with appointments he made to meet people. Soon enough no one took him seriously for anything. He lost his leadership. He lost trust. He needed to live what he preached.

3. **Confidence.** My favorite verse is: "I can do all things through Christ who strengthens me" (Phil. 4:13, NKJV). During my life, I've done lots of things because of my faith in Christ that I never would have attempted otherwise. People want to follow a leader who has confidence.

4. **Character.** The great evangelist Dwight L. Moody said, "Character is what you do in the dark." At low emotional times, temptation comes to meet legitimate needs in illegitimate ways. Instead, learn how to gain renewal of your spirit through such positive ways as rest and recreation.

5. **Courage.** I love how the Book of Joshua begins. God has to tell Joshua several times: Be courageous. The implication is that leaders will be tested. You can count on obstacles in your pathway as you lead your church from where it is to where it needs to go.

6. **Commitment.** If you are to succeed as a leader, you must be more committed than anyone else. During World War II, General Patton's troops reached a river that had no bridge. The soldiers balked at entering the freezing water. Patton himself got in, swam to the other side, waved, swam back, and then said, "Let's go." He showed that he was willing to do everything he asked them to do. He paid the cost first, and they followed. Laurie Beth Jones's book *Jesus CEO* introduces the idea of "WOWSE," which means you'll carry out a mission "with or without someone else." I wrote a book called *20/20 Vision*, which contained everything I had learned about ministry through the school of hard knocks. I had published previous books with five different publishers, but none of them wanted it. I believed so much in the book that I paid to self-publish it. Today it is still in print—in many languages as well. I was so committed to that book that I was willing to print it, believe in it, "WOWSE."

7. **Care.** Everyone at church wants to know, "Does the leader care about me?" They may love your ideas, but if they don't think you love them, they won't hear you. Showing your love is as simple as spending time to build a one-on-one relationship with them. Years ago some words from Dale Carnegie helped me, "You influence people more by listening than by talking." That's one way to help people know from their hearts that you love them.

Identifying Multiple Influencers

A little old lady named Mama Nichols was a longtime member in one of the first churches I pastored. She wasn't on any board, but she influenced the whole church. People kept going to her with prayer requests. Within days, she'd have the whole church praying about the request.

I wised up and said, "Mama Nichols, I believe this is what God wants us to do next. Would you pray with me about it?" Soon she had the whole church praying about it. She was a great influencer.

I remember serving another church when a popular staff person told me that he was going to separate from his wife. I went to our church board and no one wanted to do anything about it, so I tabled the matter, simply asking everyone to pray about it for the coming month. Meanwhile, the staff person went on a leave of absence. Before our next meeting, I talked one-on-one with 3 key influencers on the church board of 12. When we convened the meeting, they brought up the problem and talked the other members into their view. To my surprise, the vote was unanimous to ask the staff member to resign. I didn't even say a word.

Every church has a power structure. As a leader, you must learn to work with the existing structure in order to be an effective influencer. A pastor went to a large church I knew about and failed to recognize the importance of relating to the "power" people. When I inquired as to how he was getting along with certain influential people, he was quoted as saying, "Oh, I'm not going to cater to them." He chose not to spend time with them. Predictably he soon hit troubled waters. In 15 months, he was not only gone but left the church in a serious state of division.

Some leaders influence others by centering on the goal to be achieved. Known as task leader, they keep seeing the target.

Other leaders focus on building consensus. Known as cohesive leaders, they don't go forward unless everyone is, in effect, holding hands.

Early in ministry, I was extremely task-oriented. If people were upset, they'd talk to my wife because she is so approachable. She would help build consensus, and then I would lead them toward the target.

Refer to the following chart to identify up to 10 of your greatest influencers. Try to peg their style. See if you can name some ways to increase your influence on them.

Top Ten Identified Influencers

Influential person's name	Leadership style: (T) task or (C) cohesive	Who does the person influence?	How much influence? (1-10)	Is the influence positive or negative?	My influence with influencers (1-10)	How to improve my influence with this influencer

Increasing Your Influence

You never lead people farther than you're willing to go yourself. You will gain more credibility and influence as you keep learning.

What skills will you learn over the years? Learn where to be firm and where to be flexible. Keep the main thing the main thing. Be steadfast and reliable. Major on the majors. When you make a mistake, admit it and ask for forgiveness. Then keep on learning. "Patience and perseverance will accomplish more in this world than a brilliant dash," said Dale Carnegie, author of *How to Win Friends and Influence People*.

The best way to handle opponents is to treat them in a positive way. Do everything you can to turn an enemy into a friend. Always treat your critics as you would want to be treated.

Be careful not to lend any support that gives antagonists a voice to the congregation. Never surrender your leadership to negative-thinking people.

Be a pastor to them, but don't increase their influence as leaders. Remember what happened to Moses, who was among the greatest leaders in the history of Israel. How different history may have turned out if only Caleb and Joshua had reported on their visit to the Promised Land. They gave a positive, faith-filled report. Instead, after the other 10 negative reporters paralyzed the people with a we're-small-as-grasshoppers complex (see Num. 13:33), even Moses, with all his skills, couldn't move them. Negative influencers wield tremendous power.

Instead, use your influence to support the positive influencers. Decrease the leadership of the negative influencer and increase the leadership of the positive influencer. At all times, keep the focus of the church on the vision for the future and what God is doing.

In leading a church to where it needs to go, you cannot succeed if you provide backing to negative influencers. If you have a say about nominations, or if you're going to choose teachers or speakers, be careful not to give these people a platform.

As you identify your leaders, you'll quickly see that some can go either way—with the church's vision or against it. Those people are crucial to spend time with, because you can help tip the scale for them.

Also take the time to develop new influencers in your church. This takes planning and strategy. It is an ongoing process. Use the influence you have to help the up-and-coming positive influencers find the platform they need to increase their influence.

Most important, if you build leaders, they will build God's church. Leaders know how to involve others. The greatest kind of leadership is being able to influence these who in turn influence everyone else.

7

BECOMING A LEADER OF LEADERS—OF LEADERS

To make a greater difference beyond the walls of your congregation, you must go beyond a "hired hand" approach to ministry. When the paid pastor is the primary caregiver to everyone, the ministry of the church will always be limited. Pastors who think in terms of having to personally care for everyone restrict both their own ministry and that of the people of God.

Leading New Hope Community Church from zero to 6,400 members over 23 years required me to change at every stage of the church's development. Something inside me had to grow before the congregation as a whole could increase or go on to the next level.

One of the hardest privileges to give up was that of going to every meeting and knowing every member by name or face. When I was young in ministry, someone told me, "What gets your attention gets you." I decided to follow the pattern I believe comes from our Lord: pouring myself into a small group of others, who in turn can reproduce themselves. As Robert Coleman points out in the *Master Plan of Evangelism*, the initial objective of Jesus' plan was to enlist disciples who could develop not only themselves but others as well.

Learning from the Jethro Principle

Jethro, Moses' father-in-law, had been observing Moses and readily recognized that the people-care among the Israelites was extremely limited because it came primarily from one person—Moses. Jethro pointed out several problems in Moses' approach. My book *The Small Group Book* (Galloway with Mills, 1995, 85-87) explains the problems Jethro saw and the advantages of his advice:

Burnout. As a young pastor, I thought that the more hours I worked, the better a pastor I was. I have since discovered that this is not necessarily true. Jethro's advice taught me how to accomplish more in less time by keeping my span of care more limited. It also helped me share the privileges of doing ministry with many more people.

Dissatisfaction. Years ago I mistakenly thought God could use me to meet everyone's needs. So did Moses. Yet Jethro told Moses that his lone ranger approach to ministry was leaving people dissatisfied. Same in churches I served.

Unhealthiness. Moses created an unhealthy dependence on himself as leader. The people came to him for everything. I saw that happen when I went for a lunch appointment with one of my pastor friends. I arrived early and sat outside his office to wait for him. Several other people were also there waiting. After an hour of watching people go in and out of his office, I walked down the hall to check on his associate pastor. He was sitting at his desk watching a ballgame and drinking a soda. When my friend was finally free, I asked him over lunch what his associate pastor did. He smiled and answered, "I'm still trying to figure that out!"

The central idea behind Jethro's advice was to decentralize, a fancy word for shared ministry. This means you quit trying to do it all yourself and you get the ministry back to the grass roots—back to God's people where it belongs. He advised Moses to change his ministry in six ways, according to Exod. 18:13-27:

1. **Select** (v. 21). Choose capable leaders.
2. **Train** (v. 20). Teach them the laws and how to live.
3. **Organize** (v. 21). Organize them in manageable groups.
4. **Set Up a Chain of Care** (v. 22). Jethro advised Moses to let the other judges take care of the easier problems and bring only the most difficult ones to him.
5. **Delegate** (v. 22). A pastor let me preach a sermon in his church when I was 17 years old, and that's how I learned to preach. We need to do the same with releasing people for ministry: they learn ministry by doing it, but only if we leaders give them the opportunity to learn it.
6. **Achieve Balance in Life.** Moses began to seek balance in his life. By making the five changes listed above, Moses now had time for God, for his family, and for himself.

Learning to Overcome Our Insecurities

The fact that Moses took his father-in-law's advice and put the principle into practice shows that Moses was secure enough to listen to the advice of others. Are we as secure?

Eph. 4:11-13 teaches that the proper relationship between clergy and laity is a partnership in ministry. The clergy are the coaches, modeling ministry while they teach others. The people of the church are the team members, learning ministry through on-the-job training.

Leadership development is essential to all church health. As others succeed in ministry, you also become a more successful leader. Are you willing to grow in God's love and become so secure in that love that you truly begin to free others in ministry and rejoice in their successes? Insecurity is the biggest problem that keeps leaders from genuinely sharing the ministry.

Learning to Share Ministry

Build leaders, and they will build ministries. Good sharing of responsibility enhances a Christian's worth, value, and self-esteem. The following four words summarize the necessary factors in this kind of delegating:

Assignment: People need to agree to and accept the ministry you wish to release to them. According to Peter Drucker, a key question to ask is "For what are you willing to be responsible?"

Authority: People need to know that they have an authority in ministry. They also need to know the appropriate limitations to that authority.

Accountability: People don't want to feel abandoned. They need to know that an accountability system exists to support and help them.

Availability: If a person's span of care is for more than 10 people in a ministry (as illustrated in the Jethro principle), that person is probably trying to take on too much, just as Moses did.

Another Fruit: Growing Your Own Staff

Most of the staff pastors at New Hope were home-grown from laypeople raised up into leadership. Early in the life of the church, if I made a hospital call, I'd bring a potential leader with me. I'd show those in training what to do. The next time a hospital need arose, they made the visit. I lived in two worlds: doing ministry and also transferring it.

Every time I met someone or led a group, I'd be praying for God's help to develop their full ministry potential. As a result, it became natural to want to bring others along in *their* ministries.

My focus was to train in stages. If they did well in one responsibility, I'd take them to the next level. People learn ministry by doing ministry.

I remember getting together a group of 12 laymen. As we met every week, I'd find ways to share ministry with them. I had some take turns speaking on Sunday nights. Others would lead small groups. Still others would make calls on people. Out of that group eventually came a couple of full-time staff pastors.

Achieving Maximum-Impact Ministry

Would you say you spend more time: (1) developing your own leadership? (2) developing other leaders in your church? (3) developing leaders who develop leaders?

This three-step concept helps us see how to grow through these categories so we can spend more time in third-level leadership. Authentic leaders will always spend some time in hands-on ministry activities. They will also learn to work on two levels at once. For example, while providing personal pastoral care, we can recruit, train, motivate, and involve other people in doing ministry. We also learn that preaching isn't just speaking; it's leading a church by preaching.

As you develop people into leaders, and then into leaders of leaders, amazing things happen. Here is how Stephen Covey summarizes the change that occurs: "When you fully empower people, your paradigm of yourself changes. You no longer control others; they control themselves. You become a source of help to them."

If you really want to help others, then tune your barometer of effectiveness to this question: "How much time today will I invest in developing leaders of leaders?

8

USING THE ONE-STEP PRINCIPLE FOR DEVELOPING LEADERS

Jesus Christ demonstrated a simple, reproducible pattern of leadership: He concentrated on a few to get maximum results. Jesus focused His earthly ministry on a prayerfully selected small group of followers. Discipled by the Son of God and empowered by the Holy Spirit, these individuals transformed the world as they spread the life-changing good news of forgiveness, hope, and eternal life.

How did Jesus train this small band of future leaders? He did it one step at a time:

Modeling—*I do it.* "Jesus went into Galilee, proclaiming the good news" (Mark 1:14).

Mentoring—*I do it; you are with me.* "Follow me" (Mark 1:17).

Monitoring—*You do it; I am with you.* "I will make you fishers of men" (Mark 1:17).

Empowering—*You do it.* "He appointed twelve . . . that he might send them out to preach and to have authority to drive out demons" (Mark 3:14-15).

Multiplying—*You do it, and someone else is with you.* "He sent them out two by two and gave them authority" (Mark 6:7).

The application for today is clear: Build leaders, and leaders will build ministries. If you will follow Jesus' pattern, your church will follow a pathway of great fruitfulness and effectiveness. As John Maxwell says, "In order to be effective we must nurture all, equip many, and develop a few."

Be Intentional

Leadership development doesn't happen by chance. You must plan for it. Almost all of the 200 ministries at New Hope Community Church were grown by leaders we had intentionally developed.

In my mind, I regularly saw a set of stairs called leadership development.

"How do I move the person I'm developing from one step to the next step?" This question shaped everything I did, both with lay leaders and paid staff.

It seems that Jesus spent 75 to 80 percent of His time training key leaders in this way. My goal as a pastor was to follow that pattern.

Start Early

What is your master plan for developing leaders in your local church? In answering that question, do you find yourself thinking only about those who are currently serving in leadership roles?

Many pastors look over the congregations they serve and then lament, "We just don't have the kind of leaders that other congregations do." Often the problem lies in pastors limiting their view to those *already* developed as leaders. That's a common misconception. Instead of noticing what kind of leaders people are, ask God what they could become! Get them on the stairway of leadership development and see what happens.

Make it your constant habit to say, "Susan, would you make this phone call to invite this person to the group?" and "Bob, I see you like to pray; would you lead us in closing prayer?" In sharing ministry like this, you're developing people, even if they don't realize it yet.

In one of the churches I started, I wrote down the names of 12 men and then asked each, "Would you meet with me every Thursday night? I'd like to disciple you and develop you to be a leader." Most of them were new Christians. Every time I went to the hospital or made a social call to a church member, I took one of these people with me. It added time, but it multiplied ministry. Then as the church grew, I used the small-group ministry to systematically develop even more leaders.

You can develop leaders this way in every size church. As you shepherd their development, pay attention to three areas: spiritual formation; doing ministry; and becoming healthy, whole persons.

Fill the Steps

In one small group I led was a man with great potential named Rich. I gave him various responsibilities. One week when I was away, he led the discussion. Upon my return the people said, "We had better discussion with Rich than with you." I was pleased.

I worked with Rich, and it wasn't long before he started a group of his own. Later he became our church's half-time staff person in evangelism. He eventually became a pastor of single adults, leading a ministry of 800 people.

Rich matured in his ministry by going forward one step at a time. In a dynamic New Testament church, you should have people on every "step" of leadership development. No one starts at the top. Rather, people reach their full potential one step at a time. It requires an intentional plan, or it won't happen in most cases.

In fact, if the church members see only elitists on the topmost step, they won't know how to get there themselves. One of the big holdbacks to lay mobilization is an elitist complex. If laypersons feel that only a professional can do a particular type of ministry, they might never aspire to it or try to get there.

Keep Growing

Are you growing as a leader? Is God stretching you (or pruning you), teaching you new things, pushing you beyond your comfort zone, and pressing you to know and trust Him as never before? The Bible says, "To aspire to leadership is an honourable ambition" (1 Tim. 3:1, NEB).

David Durey, a staff pastor at New Hope Community Church, says, "We can impress people at a distance, but we can only impact them up close." The more you experience personal growth, the greater your potential impact will be with those you mentor. Your growth will influence their eagerness to experience multiplied ministry impact in their own lives.

Make Leaders, Not Followers

Some leaders want to make followers; I want to make leaders. My friend Rick Warren, in his book *The Purpose-Driven Church*, presents a great challenge to pastors when he says, "A great commitment to the Great Commandment and to the Great Commission will grow a great church" (102).

Ordinary people accomplish extraordinary things with the Holy Spirit.

Is that what God is calling you to do? Whatever the mind can conceive and you have the faith to believe, with God's help you can achieve. Ordinary people accomplish extraordinary things with the Holy Spirit. Your congregation and community are full of such people. What will you do next to fill that set of stairs called leadership development?

9

RELATIONAL LEADERSHIP

In recent years it seems that books on leadership are everywhere you turn. Both the business world and the church show great interest in how to develop better leadership.

One widespread model of leadership is top-down and authoritative. Lately the "in" concept is team-based leadership, where everyone has a hand in decision making.

I see a third style. It's not dictatorial, where you tell people what to do. Nor is it democratic in the sense that everyone sits around and votes. Rather, it's leader-centered. You develop leaders, and in turn they form teams and launch ministries.

All ministry is relational. Ministry can't take place unless one person reaches out to another person. For ministry to have direction and purpose, you need a leader. Without a leader you have chaos and confusion.

The following perspectives will help maximize the relational impact of your leadership style. They will help you fine-tune several delicate balances that must be considered for effective relationship-based leadership.

1. Balance Vision with Mutual Respect

The visionary leader sees the big picture. Vision gives ministry its focus. Without vision, ministry lacks a sense of direction and movement. But the ability to see and describe the next stage of ministry does not mean that the visionary leader has the better gifts.

My wife has a better sense of gut feeling than I do. I've always been good at seeing possibilities in people whom others have given up on. I know how to believe in people, which is an asset, but the trade-off is that I don't see their weaknesses as clearly as I should. I've learned to defer to Margi's wisdom.

In the early days of New Hope Community Church, which we planted together shortly after our marriage, I asked Margi to serve as church secretary. The work relationship didn't work because it was so different from what our life was like at home. In the church office, the relationship was clearly top-down: I wanted Margi to get my work done. Outside the church office, I wanted to yield to her lead in the areas that she knew best.

When we figured out what was happening, we hired someone else to work as church secretary. We soon learned how to work well together in the church by having mutual respect for one another's abilities and the areas each of us led. Practicing the "submit to one another" concept of Eph. 5:21, we each submitted to whatever the other knew most, both in ministry and in marriage. Through relational ministry, we each developed and grew, and the people we worked with had more effective leadership as a result.

This "submit to one another" concept works well in ministry. Somebody has to be the leader of a team, but administratively you don't want to make decisions without involving the people who know the most about it.

This attitude is why I have avoided the term *assistant* pastor and instead have given this staff member an area of responsibility. Doing so helps build respect for this person's area of expertise.

You want to empower leaders to do everything they can do at their level. You're trusting them. In my view it's the most Christian way of leadership because it recognizes people's giftedness, it builds them up, values them, and brings the best decisions. Those closest to the scene will know what's best for the situation.

2. Balance Individuality with Teamwork

Leaders have a sense of task and purpose, but they must never promote a lone ranger attitude. They understand that people are interconnected and that no one should do ministry alone.

Consider the beautiful picture of relationships in ministry we see in the Trinity. One of Christianity's distinctives is our view of one God as three Persons. The members of the Godhead communicate with each other. They represent unity in diversity. Each member of the Trinity serves as a model of relational ministry with the other members.

The Bible's instruction about the Church as the Body of Christ emphasizes that every member has something of value to contribute. It says we need each other. In fact, it tells us something is wrong with our attitude if we think or say otherwise. "The eye cannot say to the hand, 'I don't need you!' And the head cannot say to the feet, 'I don't need you!'" (1 Cor. 12:21).

3. Balance Firmness with Flexibility

Good leaders learn to discern when to be firm and when to be flexible. You need to be flexible when something doesn't detract from the vision or purpose, but firm when it does. Leaders are flexible about ideas that build people and accomplish good things, but firm when people need boundaries and direction. Leaders are firm when something will violate agreed-on core values and when certain behaviors will take people away from the main thing.

Wherever possible, however, let the leader grow it and build it. Healthy decentralization multiplies ministry while it develops people who have demonstrated they are leaders by the way they handle responsibility.

As a leader you set the vision and boundaries under a big umbrella so people will have lots of room to dream their dreams and not feel boxed in. Otherwise, if you take away their role in decision making, you will deflate and devalue them.

4. Balance "Reveal" with "Conceal"

In a past era you might listen to an entire series of sermons, teachings, or training and never hear one personal illustration. You would have no idea how the message had impacted the messenger.

Communicators today tend to include many stories and experiences from their own spiritual journey. Vulnerability and authenticity are very important to effective communication in the 21st century.

Yet there is a balance. If you overreveal your dirty laundry, you lose respect as a leader. You can create backlash without meaning to.

Remember when Jimmy Carter commented to an interviewer that he had lusted after women other than his wife? Probably every normal man in history has lusted. But the way he said it invited misunderstanding.

A vital question: what to reveal and what to conceal? As you share your struggles in being authentic, be sure to emphasize how God has brought you through to victory. If you tell stories about yourself to fulfill your own ego needs, people will not want to follow you. If your point is to show how God has worked in the circumstances of your life, then you may find many people eager to travel the journey with you. As the apostle Paul said, "Therefore I glory in Christ Jesus in my service to God. I will not venture to speak of anything except what Christ has accomplished through me" (Rom. 15:17-18).

5. Balance Hierarchy with Servant Leadership

Strong dictatorial leadership tends to make people feel like children. Their judgment is not valued. People with leadership ability will rebel against this kind of authoritarian leadership, or they will go to another church. They want to be treated as persons of value.

Servant leaders value people. They are relational. They do not make decisions apart from consulting with other key leaders. They make decisions based on what's best for the whole family. They take seriously the command, "Be devoted to one another in brotherly love. Honor one another above yourselves" (Rom. 12:10).

How can you tell if you are modeling servant

Traps That Hinder Relational Ministry

Insecurity: Selecting only those people who have the same gifts as the leader—or lesser gifts.

Elitism: Developing a "leaders only" attitude that keeps one from sharing responsibility with others.

Codependency: Making decisions not motivated solely on what's best for others.

Control Issues: Staying wrapped up in one's own power needs.

Immaturity: Caring more about themselves as leaders than others.

Lack of Trust: Conveying the idea that they don't trust the people they're trying to empower.

leadership? You're never any better than the leadership you've developed. Are the team leaders you're cultivating more concerned about their own power and control issues or about doing what's best for the rest of the group?

If you build leaders, they'll build the groups that build ministries.

How do you minimize hierarchy? You keep things as simple as possible. You find people who know the most about an area and you make them the leader. Then they build a team around it. It's as simple—and hard—as that.

The bottom line of this chapter can be summarized in one sentence: *If you build leaders, they'll build the groups that build ministries.* Those ministries, in turn, will be built on the values of mutual respect, teamwork, flexibility, authenticity, and servant leadership.

You want to maximize people because leaders lead people. The people you shape will in turn cultivate and advance others. That's a wonderful pathway to bring out the best in everyone.

You'll also receive a great personal payback. One of the greatest joys you will ever know comes from developing people to become stronger leaders.

10

HARNESSING THE BIG "M" (MOMENTUM)

The New York Central Railway Company claimed that its largest locomotive, thundering down the tracks at top speed, could crash through concrete five feet thick. That same train on public display was held in place by a one-inch block. What made the difference? Momentum.

When sufficient momentum swells in a church, the congregation becomes unstoppable. The members believe God for the impossible. They become excited about bringing their neighbors into the life of Christ's Body. They find great spiritual joy in being involved in a cause that's greater than the humdrum activities of daily life.

How to Identify It

Momentum is a belief that transcends the everyday into the extraordinary. According to Alan Nelson, "Momentum is often like the magical pixie dust that transforms ordinary people into superheroes, and otherwise mundane events and activities into divine phenomena."

Momentum originates in the power of the Holy Spirit. It is the result of the whole church's buying into a positive attitude of faith.

There's a certain mystery about momentum, just as there is about the Holy Spirit. Yet most leaders can quickly recognize when they have momentum and when they don't—even if they're not quite sure how it got there!

How to Create It

Leaders must not only understand momentum but also know how to create it. Heb. 11 provides a vivid illustration of how to produce faith-building momentum: You center on marvelous things that God has done and will do. Similarly, a Christian can't read the Book of Acts without being caught up in the momentum of something great happening in the Church.

Faith is seeing something before it becomes reality. Without that kind of vision, you won't have momentum. Similarly, without passion for souls, you'll lack momentum. If you focus on negative circumstances and all that's wrong, you'll look in vain for momentum.

Instead, a pastor generates momentum by keeping the church focused on what God wants to do, not by getting bogged down in the junk. In other words, see it big and keep it simple.

The leader is the person able to focus the congregation on God and what God wants to accomplish. Elmer Towns says, "When they buy into your dream, they buy into your leadership."

As a leader, you have to be more like a thermostat than a thermometer. A thermometer simply measures, but a thermostat sets the climate. A church leader functions as a thermostat by

- Casting a vision of faith
- Focusing people on God
- Sharing testimonies of what God is doing through
- Helping people live in positive expectation of future events planned for their church
- Being enthusiastic about everything God has done to date
- Believing God for the impossible in the future

As a leader, be optimistic. Express enthusiasm. Plant dreams in the spirit of your congregation. Spark fires in members' hearts. Lead them into further positive experiences by putting "wins" under their belts. As you equip people for ministry along the way, you will build momentum.

Certain times of the year, such as Easter and Christmas, readily lend themselves to creating momentum. Church milestones and corporate spiritual victories can also provide launchpads for producing momentum.

When I was pastoring, I looked year-round for fresh ways to spark momentum. If I couldn't find an immediate example, I'd simply state, "This is the First Church of Where It's Happening." As a result, during my pastoral experience of 32 years, only about 3 or 4 years were not characterized by momentum.

How to Build It

Leaders understand and consciously build momentum. You build and multiply it by centering on the positive and ignoring the negative.

If you want to build momentum, get your people praying.

When Margi and I started New Hope Community Church, we had no people, no money, and no building. We met rain or shine in an outdoor drive-in theater, preaching on top of the snack shack roof and trying to sing along with prerecorded organ music that was regularly miscued by one of our previously unchurched helpers. (Since he had never been to church before, he couldn't recognize songs by their tunes.)

We could have talked about what we didn't have, but instead we emphasized what we had: lives being transformed. There's nothing like a changed life to build momentum. Celebrative worship also helps build momentum. Small-group community likewise helps build it. Spiritual happenings create strong momentum. So do statements of faith like "Someday God is going to . . ."

If you want to build momentum, get your people praying. Fill your sermons with positive affirmations like "Nothing is impossible with God." Then watch how God uses that environment to build confidence in what He will do through you.

Momentum, like a snowball, feeds on itself, picking up more and more ground as it moves along. The excitement about church bubbles over as your people bring more people and those newcomers introduce the church to their friends.

Leaders are perceived to be better than they are when they have high momentum and worse than they are when they have low momentum. When you don't have momentum, the stuff of life tends to take over.

How to Use It

"Momentum to an organization is like adrenaline to the human body," says Alan Nelson. It helps you turn corners and handle surprises that might otherwise cause trauma and insurmountable hurdles.

Once leaders know how to create and build momentum, they can use it to bring about needed change. For instance, successfully relocating a church or changing the style of worship is impossible without momentum.

I currently worship at Southland Christian Church, a thriving congregation in Lexington, Kentucky. The new senior minister, Mike Breaux, whose respected predecessor Wayne Smith had been there 40 years, hit the ground running when he came. During his first year he implemented many changes designed to make it more seeker-friendly. Both the worship and the preaching styles went through major adjustments.

This newcomer from Nevada, with the blessing of the previous minister, was successful in the transition because he had the momentum. The church was excited and attendance increased. "Momentum is the greatest of all change agents," says author and communicator John Maxwell.

One of Robert Schuller's books is called *Peak-to-Peek Principle*. It describes building on one point and from there using the ground gained to stretch for the next peak. This approach enables maximum stewardship of momentum.

Similarly, John Maxwell wrote a book called *Success Journey*. One of its implications is that if you get a church living together to build a dream, you'll have positive momentum.

How to Kill It

Momentum is no respecter of church size or church finances. If you're not a good steward of momentum, you lose it. With momentum, people follow the leader. They're excited and bring other people. Without it, they hesitate, become distracted, and too often become critical. Momentum dies when people lose confidence in a leader.

If you're living on yesterday's successes, your momentum is dying.

In smaller churches, one major problem can distract everyone's focus, while in larger churches it's hard for one issue to kill forward progress. Instead, only when five or six problems come together in a short period of time will momentum be negatively affected. In bigger churches momentum is like a big ship; it may be slow to gain speed, but it's hard to stop once it starts moving.

When you don't have momentum, people will center on insignificant things. Bad attitudes become more predominant, people's problems grow bigger, and people pick on each other as well as the pastor.

Success is an unending process. Whenever a church thinks it has arrived, the momentum will slacken. If you're living on yesterday's successes, your momentum is dying and you don't even know it.

How to Bridge It

In the early 1970s, a pastor I knew went through a tragic divorce. Yet that year ended with the highest attendance and conversion gain that this 75-year-old church had ever experienced. How was this possible? All the momentum built from previous years took several months to be killed by the fallout from the marital breakup.

Ken Blanchard's book *Mission Possible* talks of CEOs living in two worlds: improving the present paradigm now while also living in the future, creating the new paradigm.

Effective pastors today must learn to live in both worlds, improving the present world while planning for the future one. Start where you are and be realistic. At the same time expect great things from God and do great things for Him. You will be surprised by all that can happen as you build confidence in what God is going to do.

11

Building a Dream Team

Coaching, mentoring, and cheerleading—these wonderful development roles have moved to front and center of organizations, business enterprises, and institutions like hospitals and schools. The concept means every leader has privilege and responsibility to develop other people.

The terms may be new, but the idea of leadership development has been happening in the church since the time of Jesus. We learned it from our Leader. Mentoring for effective ministry is what Jesus did for three years with His disciples. Coaching His followers on how to make the maximum impact for righteousness in their world has stood at the center of our Lord's work for 2,000 years. His cheerleading makes ministry incredibly enjoyable most of the time, and His approval makes it bearable all the other times.

In giving specific attention to the senior pastor's task to coach, mentor, and cheerlead staff and lay leaders, three significant dimensions seem to warrant the highest priority. Those three elements are to (1) love your team members, (2) communicate the vision over and over until it becomes crystal clear to all you lead, and (3) trust your team to help carry heavy parts of your load.

Mentor Through Unconditional Love

The effective Christian leads with love. President Eisenhower once said, "You do not lead by hitting people over the head. Any fool can do that, but it is usually called assault, not leadership." In conscientiously mentoring your church staff, you earn the right to be followed by the way you love them. If they know you love them, they will follow you almost anywhere.

Live by the passage "Put love first" (1 Cor. 14:1, NEB). Loving your staff is always more important than any program. It is even more important than having your way. It is a thousand times more important than showing your staff who is boss. Effective senior pastors, as chief of staff, learn to love people any way they find them.

When staff mess up, love them to wholeness. Make the choice to love in the way Christ loved His disciples. Put Christ's love into practice, and watch it work through your staff, lay leaders, and congregation. Love people enough to forgive them before they ask or if they never ask. Choose to love and eat humble pie in your relationships with the staff and lay leaders if that is what it takes to live in peace and keep harmony in the church.

Staff members learn to love by watching you. View your love for them as an investment in their growth and as a teaching model for their ministry. Love always wins in every situation.

When staff and lay leaders know you love and value them, they will do almost anything for you. People always work harder for praise and love than they do for more money.

Coach Through Constant Communication of Vision

Most staff members joined your team originally because they believed in your vision. Some of them are there only because you are the leader.

Some pastors keep power in their hands by keeping their staff and lay leaders uninformed. Big mistake. Leaders who withhold information put staff in compromised situations because they do not know the whole story about an issue. A wise old pastor told me, "Withholding information from those who need it to do their work is just plain wicked." Be sure to live by the golden rule of communication: keep others informed in the way you wish to be kept informed.

Tell your staff over and over about your dreams for the church. Tell them often about your hopes for their individual ministries. Listen to what they are thinking. Provide answers to issues that confuse them. If they are waiting for an answer from a decision group, give them the report as soon as possible. Express appreciation for their work. Tell them how well they are doing in front of other staff members. Be gentle, patient, and kind for Jesus' sake.

Trust Them to Help Carry Heavy Loads

Staff people cannot bear all the senior pastor's pressures all the time, but they can help more times than we think. Trust them to help you carry a heavy load. They will feel involved, needed, and close to you.

Keep asking yourself, "What am I carrying that I need to learn to shoulder together with others?" This does not constitute a selfish request, nor is it an expression of weakness. It is the lifeblood of empowered ministry and biblical community. Your health and well-being may depend on it. The staff's professional growth and spiritual development depend on it too.

The Ultimate Result of a Good Team

Coach Paul "Bear" Bryant grew great football teams when they "got one heartbeat together." The same is true with church teams. A "one heartbeat together" church staff team composed of a player-coach pastor, a staff that shares the same dream, and a solid core of trained lay leaders working together can build a great church.

I have given serious thought to what the Bible requires a great church to be and what contemporary people look for in a church. I believe the two lists are not so different. My short list of what the Bible requires is that a church provide (1) worship, so every attender is aware of God in all of life; (2) a salvation message, so every unbeliever knows where and how to find the Savior—and at the same time causes every believer to rejoice in the new life Christ provides for them; (3) belonging and fellowship, so everyone has an effective support system of caring friends; (4) discipleship, nurture, and edification, so believers fully understand the implications of their faith; (5) accountability, so all believers can accept responsibility for their conduct and attitudes; and (6) ministry or service, so everyone has an easily recognized way to exercise the gifts God has given each one.

Doesn't that list sound a lot like what many contemporary people seek? Aren't they asking questions about a Supreme Being? Aren't they seeking the meaning of life that salvation brings? Aren't they looking for a place to belong for support and acceptance? Don't they need an accountability relationship to persons they can trust? Don't they need a place where they can give themselves to a great cause?

Think about it. When you build a great staff who in turn release God's people to build ministry, then spiritual and emotional needs are met for everyone—staffers, volunteers, Joe and Jane Christian in the pew, and the senior pastor in the center of it all. It also attracts unbelievers. Lay ministry may be the way to make the church more viable than ever before in human history.

I love this lay ministry summary from *The Living Body*, by Richard Halverson, former chaplain of the United States Senate: "The church of Jesus Christ does not make its maximum impact on the world through its so-called professionals—preachers, pastors, evangelists, missionaries, directors of Christian education. It makes its greatest impact through its laypeople. It is through the people of God, in whom Christ dwells by His Spirit, that He speaks His word and does His work. The people of God influence the world for Christ wherever He has sent them, wherever He has planted them. Through His people, Christ is infiltrating all the units of society throughout the earth" (1994, 125).

The real test of whether you've built a dream-team staff, is whether the people of God are having a maximum possible impact on each other and on the culture around them.

When you develop others as members of a team with you, you always have to give up something. But you always gain far more in the process. More important, the size of dream your church can accomplish will be far greater than you could ever hope to tackle alone.

12

CHECKLIST FOR A STRONG STAFF TEAM

The larger the staff grows, the more time you need to spend together in relating, bonding, and becoming a team. It is hard but satisfying work. Doing it well multiplies your effectiveness and your own sense of achievement. These 21 tips show how a senior pastor can better relate to the staff team.

1. Model

Every team requires a leader. Model what you want them to be and do. This modeling concept applies to the time you arrive at work, use of time during the day, your days off, your stewardship, and even the way you treat people. Do not ask a staff person to do what you are not willing to do. Model whatever you are trying to accomplish.

2. Build Success

Help each staff member be successful. Helping people achieve their best is the most satisfying part of leading a staff team. Ask yourself, "Do I set people up for success, or for failure?" A real leader helps others succeed. That happens best as I commit to do everything I can to develop every staff member. That is part of my stewardship to God as senior pastor.

3. Be Fair

Be fair in recognition and compensation. It is unfair for a senior pastor to be way ahead of everyone else in salary and perks. Financial compensation means more than dollars; it shows a church's priorities and values. A finance committee may say to you, "Pastor, we would like to give you a big raise. We think you deserve it." That's the time for you to say, "We have staff people who really need the money more." Be realistic.

Obviously, senior pastors should be adequately paid for their work and responsibility. But your fairness is questioned and staff morale is destroyed if you say, "We are a team together," when you keep taking more money and more benefits while everyone else is forced to live on a much lower scale. If you want to build a strong team, you have to be fair about compensation for those who serve with you. Keep in mind, a 5 percent raise is a lot more new money on a $60,000 scale than it is on a $20,000 scale. Staff members can do the math just as well as you can.

4. Encourage

Encouragement is among the biggest things anyone in ministry needs. One friend of mine who is a successful senior pastor made it a practice when he saw the spouse of a staff member in a hallway at church to ask, "How is your husband doing?" or "How is your wife doing?" Their reply would help him spot discouragement quickly. When he discovered a problem, he went to work on it.

5. Require Accountability

Hold each staff member accountable. Accountability is often missing in the contemporary church because we do not focus on results of mission or achievement. Sadly, too many persons in ministry fool themselves into thinking they are working hard at what matters when they are actually wasting their time on trivia. To really make accountability work, the pastor will have some level of accountable to the staff.

I like to manage by objective, so I asked each staff member to set goals, write them down, and hand them in. Then on a weekly report sheet, I asked, "What is it that you are doing in your ministry to meet your goals for the next month? What is it you are working on for this month?" Some pastors use the weekly staff meetings for reports of accountability.

6. Require Goals

Require each staff person to set ministry goals. Help them set goals for their personal long-term development and for their own ministry. Teach them how to set short-range, middle-range, and long-range goals. Goals help a staffer achieve greater things for God and the church. At the same time, they do something significant for the individual. Allan Cox explains how they work in his book, *Straight Talk for Monday Morning*: "They [goals] let us know we're heading in the right direction and are exhilarating in their own right. They are a confirmation of our strength, an expression of our growth, vitality—our authenticity. They keep us looking up, forward" (1992, 74). Goals help people grow.

7. Support

Back your staff. Establish a relationship of trust with your staff by your reactions to questions from the congregation. Let them know they can count on your support. Affirm in public and correct in private.

8. Train

Be a teacher. Model what you teach. Be willing to show staff members how to do any phase of ministry where they are inexperienced. Most ministry skills can be learned if the teacher and student learn from each other.

9. Share

Share ministry with staff members. Give staffers place and position in the church. Help them use all their spiritual gifts so they feel fulfilled. Make sure they are challenged to their full potential. When appropriate, give them platform duties like pastoral prayer and preaching. Don't be afraid to set tough standards, but be realistic in your evaluations.

10. Give Personal Attention

Spend time with each staff person. I had one-on-one breakfasts or lunches with staff persons on a fairly regular basis. If I observed someone in staff meeting gazing out the window, or if it looked as if the person was discouraged, I would set a lunchtime with him or her. My wife, Margi, is really great about picking up problems in body language that I often do not see. She was on our staff and would say to me, "I think so-and-so is having a little problem. You should get with them."

11. Repeat Yourself

Keep sharing your vision from your heart. You are the vision caster. You must recast the vision over and over. On a frequent basis, the staff needs to hear the dream directly from you. Vision forces the leader to take a stand for a preferred future. When shared and understood, the vision motivates staff members to achievement, and it becomes a word picture of what the church can become.

Management specialist Stuart R. Levine in *The Leader in You* significantly helped me with this insight, which I applied to ministry. "From day one the Apple founders kept their vision intact and they communicated it at every turn. They hired people who understood the vision and let them share in its rewards. They lived and breathed and talked the vision. Even when the company got stalled—when the retailers said no thank you, when the manufacturing people said no way, when the bankers said no more—Apple's visionary leaders never backed down" (1993, 23).

12. Be Vulnerable

Share your own needs. Be human. Be humble. Ask for their prayers. You are not God. Neither are you superman or superwoman. I went to a staff meeting one day, pulled out a chair, and shared a pressing personal need. I felt stressed throughout my whole body. The staff laid hands on me. They prayed for me—as we are instructed to do in James 5:16: "Confess your faults one to another, and pray one for another, that ye may be healed" (KJV).

My burden lifted as they prayed. Then when I got up, another pastor sat down in my place. We prayed for him, and then another. That continued for two hours. We didn't get to the staff agenda that day. But one lady on our staff said to another pastor as we left, "That is the best staff meeting we have ever had." Another person said, "I felt much closer to the pastor today than I have ever felt."

Here's how this dynamic principle works: Unless leaders are willing to humble themselves, share from their own lives, and allow other people the privilege of praying for them, it will not be easy for other staff people to admit their needs and to receive the support they need.

13. Give Others Value

Every human being has certain ego needs and sensitivities. I have an ego. You have an ego. Keep aware of the inner needs of your staff. Keep close to them. Help them grow into great servants of Christ. And above all else, practice the Golden Rule in your contacts with them. In every way possible give them the gifts of importance and significance.

14. Seek Balance

Help team members live a balanced life. I asked on the weekly report sheet, "How much time did you spend in prayer? How much time did you spend with your family, or with your spouse?" On occasion, when I observed someone's life getting out of balance, I would say, "You need to take a couple days off with your family." Or "Here is a gift certificate. Take your spouse to this fine hotel, and just get away for several days."

They may respond, "Well, what about . . . ?" Then I would say, "We will find a pinch hitter among the many people you've been training." Your church wants and needs staffers to be healthy, whole people. Ministry is always impacted by who and what a staff member is on the inside. Emotional cripples will make followers into emotional cripples.

15. Listen

Pay attention to the spirit of your staff. Listen for attitudes, hurts, and joys. Allow the team to discuss the spirit of the church and the staff. Ask for ways they think it can be improved. Collectively, they know a great deal about your church that they need to feel comfortable sharing with you.

16. Be Positive

Give every person "Triple A" treatment: attention, appreciation, and affirmation. In a regular staff meeting, I sensed something was wrong with a woman who had been on staff for a long time at New Hope Church. Something was out of sync. She opposed nearly everything anyone else proposed. Up until then, she had always been a great team player. So, when I observed this change, I went to her office, knocked on her door, went in, and sat down.

As she sat behind her desk, I said, "I just wanted to share with you how much I value your ministry. I am glad you are on this team. You know you have been here 10 years, and you have done a great job. You minister to people I cannot get close to. You have helped so many people. I thank God for you."

Then she replied with pain in her voice, "I didn't know you cared anymore."

Without trying to defend myself, I said, "Oh, I am sorry. I have taken you for granted. I really value you. You are important to all of us on this team."

Guess what—we had a prayer together, and everything was OK at the next staff meeting.

Every day when I was at the church, I walked around the building to spend a few minutes with every employee I met. Whether it was a custodian, a secretary, or a fellow staff pastor, I would look the person in the eye and say, "How are you doing today?" Such intentional tuning in makes an amazing difference in staff relationships.

I had a custodian with whom I got upset. Later, I had to go to him and say, "I am really sorry I spoke in such a rude way. I really value your hard work. I know you are always being pushed around here, and you have so much work to do. Would you please forgive me?"

He put his arm around me, patted me on the shoulder, and said, "Pastor. It's OK. Really." When I walked away, he had a big smile on his face. I could easily have said to myself, "Self, you were right. He was not doing his job." But I would have created a strained relationship that bothered us both and perhaps undermined the quality of his work.

Remember this important reality about staff relationships: Keep relationships up-to-date. Your staff may need a truckload of forgiveness with each other. But mutual forgiveness stands at the heart of the Christian faith. Sometimes it means humbling yourself and saying, "I was wrong." As you model Christlikeness, you discover other staff people will follow your example in their relationships with other staff members, with volunteers, and with the congregation.

17. Empower

Give staff members boundaries, yet provide them lots of freedom within those boundaries. Stay in control without controlling. Be flexible when you need to be flexible. Be firm when it is necessary. Effective control depends on happy past relationships. It is like putting money in the bank for a day when you really need it.

18. Be Secure

Become secure in who you are. Keep working at self-understanding so you know why you do what you do. Take time to laugh at yourself. Be comfortable with who you are. Work at being a healthy, well-balanced leader. Encourage people on your staff to be themselves.

19. Build Family

Treat your staff as brothers and sisters in Christ. It is the magnetism of Christ that brings a staff together in the first place. Never treat them as children or slaves. In an ultimate sense, they serve Christ and not you. View them as your partners in Christian service. Love them with the love of Jesus, and they will follow you anywhere.

20. Be Patient

Give your staff time to develop. An old proverb always helps me: "If you are planting for 1 year, grow rice. If you are planting for 20 years, grow trees. If you are planting for centuries, grow leaders." Think about it—if staff members were as mature and experienced as you, they would probably be serving somewhere else. So be patient as they develop, just as someone showed you long-suffering in your development phase.

21. Connect

Plan and conduct weekly staff meetings. Here is the New Hope pattern: first I met with staff pastors, and we prayed for one another and shared our spiritual life. During my final years there, this represented 18 to 20 people.

Following that meeting, we moved to a larger room where we met with all employees, including secretaries and custodians, for a half-hour devotional fellowship. We prayed with these support people, and I sometimes shared the vision of the ministry. If there were questions, we answered them. As senior pastor, I often provided ongoing teaching about ministry and spiritual life.

Then the pastoral team moved to another room where we had our regular staff meeting. There we shared information, planning, and communications. No one ever builds a great church without weekly meetings with the leadership team.

The staff meeting components included encouragement, bonding, laughter, accountability, reporting, and vision casting. Let me sound a caution—as the staff gets larger, the tendency is to spend less time together. But in a larger congregation, you need more time together rather than less.

In a large church, it became difficult to get the whole staff away for a couple of days of retreat, so we did 24-hour retreats. Sometimes we would do a daytime retreat where we would all get on a bus together, 8:00 in the morning, drive somewhere, and have the meals there that day. In retreats, it is important to leave space for fun, like playing volleyball together. I found staff retreats, even a one-day retreat, accomplish so much more closeness than we could create in a regular week-after-week staff meeting.

Rate Yourself on How You're Doing

1. Model
2. Build success
3. Be fair
4. Encourage
5. Require accountability
6. Require goals
7. Support
8. Train
9. Share
10. Give personal attention
11. Repeat yourself
12. Be vulnerable
13. Give others value
14. Seek balance
15. Listen
16. Be positive
17. Empower
18. Be secure
19. Build family
20. Be patient
21. Connect

Which of these do you do best? Where would you like to improve?

SECTION THREE

Break Free from Attitudes that Attack

13

BECOMING BROKEN TO BLESS

There are things that cannot be changed, no matter how hard you struggle." Of the 16 books I've written, the one that has been in print the longest is the account of my deepest personal crisis and how God gave me new hope through it. God has used that story to touch Christian leaders at their deepest level of pain. As I travel across North America representing the Beeson programs and speaking at conferences and seminars, I continually meet pastors and laypeople who tell me that at their point of deepest need, someone handed them that book. It has helped them break out of their shattered circumstances and become an overcomer.

Tyndale House distributed the book for 17 years under the title *Dream a New Dream* and later *Rebuild Your Life*. In 1993 I updated the book and republished it privately (it's available through 20/20 Vision, 1-800-420-2048). This chapter explains the lessons God taught me almost three decades ago. I first penned these principles in 1974, beginning with the quote above, and they continue to be foundational to my life and ministry.

1. Accept What You Cannot Change

Many facts of life cannot be changed:
- The weather
- The unrelenting tick of the clock
- The past
- The fact that a loved one has died
- Other people against their will

The unchangeable event that wrenched my life apart took place in 1970. According to my wife's preplanned time schedule, a total stranger handed me divorce papers a few days before Christmas. Within 24 hours I stood at the Portland International Airport, and through misty eyes watched helplessly as the woman I had loved, honored, and cherished since I was 18 years old led my two children onto an airplane and departed, never to return.

Life became worse than death. I had lost my marriage, my confidence in ministry, and my peace.

The most difficult thing I have ever done in my life was to come to the point of surrendering the right to be with my two children, to guide their lives, to enjoy watching them grow up, and to offer any input in how they would be raised.

The months that followed remain a blur in my memory. At one point, having lost all sense of time, I wandered aimlessly along an unknown beach, sobbing uncontrollably. I recall shouting angrily at God again and again, asking how my life could be so shattered, how someone I so loved could decide that she did not love me and that she never had.

"Commit your way to the LORD; trust in him and he will do this," says Ps. 37:5. This concept, when practiced completely, was the turning point God used to help me know what to change and what to accept.

- Acceptance means you stop fighting the inevitable.
- Acceptance stops a lot of hurt.
- Acceptance frees you not to worry about anything that is out of your power to change.
- Acceptance enables you to let go and let God. Then you will know what to leave alone and what to change, and the result will be inner serenity.

In order to begin my change into all God created me to become, I had to accept what could not be altered. Through prayer and the counsel of others, I accepted responsibility not to remain the person I was. I asked God to transform my brokenness into wholeness.

2. Stop Playing the Blame Game

John 9 tells the story of Jesus' interaction with the man who had been blind from birth. Seeing this man, the disciples demanded to know, "Who sinned, this man or his parents, that he was born blind?" (v. 2). In other words, they were asking who was to blame.

In most cases the blame game only creates injury:

- It never heals—it always hurts.
- It never makes people whole—it only breaks relationships.
- It never unites—it only divides.
- It never builds—it only tears apart.
- It never solves a problem—it only compounds the problem.

Jesus came to stop this cycle. He said, in essence, "Forget these blaming games. Ask instead, 'How can we help this man? Where does he go from here? How can we make the situation new and better?'"

As we go through life's crises, we need to guard against three harmful responses: (1) blaming God; (2) blaming others; (3) blaming yourself.

When Jesus died on the Cross, He took my failures, my sins, and my brokenness in His redemptive suffering. As I agonized over where I had gone wrong, God gave me this freeing verse: "There is now no condemnation for those who are in Christ Jesus" (Rom. 8:1). I felt as if Jesus were saying, "Go, and play the blame game no more."

3. Make the Wonderful Discovery of Who You Are

The third step in my emotional healing occurred when I learned that in God's sight, a person is neither a complete failure nor a hopeless sinner. For months, I had been going over the same ground, admitting, confessing, looking at my failings, trying to see where I had gone wrong. One day as I was driving down the freeway, I visualized Jesus hanging on a cross, crying out in despair, "My God, my God, why hast thou forsaken me?" (KJV).

The truth suddenly hit me: Whatever's wrong with me was hung on the Cross. Jesus suffered for *me*, just as Isa. 53:5 says. He took my failures, my sins, and my shortcomings.

There is no sin Jesus didn't cover. To go on punishing myself and beating myself down for something I had done wrong or failed to do right was to disregard what Jesus did for me when He took my place on the Cross. In Christ's resurrection is new hope and new life!

When I stopped blaming myself, I was able to discover even more wonders of God's amazing love. I came to see that every human is a divine original. Of all God's wondrous creations, He made people "a little lower than the angels . . . crowned . . . with glory and honour" (Ps. 8:5, KJV).

Some people have the mistaken notion that it's wrong to have good feelings about themselves. As my friend Robert Schuller says in *Move Ahead with Possibility Thinking,* "I'm really a wonderful person when Christ lives in me. I've been too self-critical. I've been my own worst enemy. I'm a child of God. God loves me. I can do all things through Christ who strengthens me" (1967, 35).

God is not finished with you or me. The best is yet to come! God wanted to turn my brokenness into a ministry of hope, using it to heal many other broken people and give them hope as well.

4. Slam the Door on Self-Pity

Self-pity is an ever-present temptation to those who are undergoing an emotionally shattering experience. It is many people's number one private enemy.

Elijah, one of the greatest prophets who ever lived, is pictured under the juniper tree singing the blues, having allowed self-pity to overtake him. Peter, one of the greatest disciples who ever lived, held a one-person pity party. He felt sorry for himself because God had laid on him the sacrificial responsibilities of Kingdom work. Ps. 73 describes a man who was pitying himself because the wicked were prospering and he was having a hard time.

Self-pity is one luxury that no one can afford. To engage in it is to hurt yourself far more than anything that has hurt you previously. Close the door on self-pity and you shut out the major cause of depression.

To get rid of self-pity, I learned to do these six things:
1. Spot it quickly and see it for what it is.
2. Exercise your power to make self-pity an unwelcome guest.
3. Make use of physical exercise.
4. Expect some heartache along the way.

5. Focus on what you have, not what you have lost.

6. Give yourself in service to others.

Paul and Silas, released from jail, went to Lydia's house to meet with other Christians (see Acts 16). They could have taken the opportunity to get everyone to feel sorry for them because they had been in prison for the Lord's work. Instead they ceased not to teach and preach Jesus Christ. Since self-pity is a direct result of self-centeredness, there is no better cure than giving oneself to others.

5. Apply Healing Medicine to Your Emotional Wounds

Jesus was rejected, lied against, betrayed by close friends, and unable to get even His mother to understand why He must die. Not once did He strike back at those who brought Him physical suffering or emotional pain.

Jesus was hurt that we might be healed. If we go on hurting emotionally long after our injury, then we have no one to blame but ourselves. To heal the bitterness and pain of a wounded spirit, I learned to take these seven steps:

1. Tell yourself that no one can hurt you any more than you allow.

2. Open yourself to God for cleaning out the wound.

3. Practice forgiveness.

4. Pray for anyone who despitefully uses you.

5. Give others the benefit of the doubt, even those who hurt you.

6. Let God heal your broken spirit.

7. Overcome evil by doing good.

6. Choose and Cultivate a Positive Attitude

The following motto, called the Achiever's Creed, is based on Phil. 4:13:

Whatever the mind can conceive
and I will dare to believe,
with God's help, I can achieve.

Holocaust survivor Viktor Frankl learned a valuable lesson as enemy soldiers took all his earthly possessions—his clothes, his watch, and even his wedding ring. As he stood naked, his body shaved, he was destitute but for one thing. It was something no one could take from him. He realized in that moment that he still had the power to choose his own attitude.

I am not responsible for the attitudes and actions of anyone but myself. No matter what happens, the attitude choice is still yours or mine.

7. Love Again, Only More

Open any newspaper today and you will find stories of people stirred to hate, despair, and senseless violence. People today desperately need God's love, the only medicine for the sickness of this world.

Without love, we perish. If you have love, you have everything. Only a love like God's can bring the very best out of us. With God's help, your love can be as beautiful as you make it.

All my life I have been highly goal-oriented. My lifetime goal has been to build a great church for the unchurched. To achieve this goal, I gave time, energy, and money. It was a worthy goal that brought out the best in me. However, it is also where I failed most in my first marriage. As God-honoring as it is to build a church with multiple ministries to thousands of people, it was also my point of marital failure.

In my emotional brokenness, I resolved instead to make love my number one aim. My first goal today, my highest goal that makes my life so much more meaningful today than yesterday, is love. Love always wins.

8. Put Your Failure Behind You and Move Ahead

The negative thinker says failure is a disgrace, failure occurs when a person doesn't achieve, and failure is final. Through my darkest moments, God showed me that people are created for something far greater than to be bearers of a failure complex. Instead, we are to profit from our mistakes and move ahead with new determination:

- To fail is not to be a failure.
- To err is human.
- No one is a failure who tries.
- Failure need never be final.

History records the story of Thomas Edison's efforts to develop the light bulb. His first 6,000 experiments were unsuccessful. One day when someone asked him if he was discouraged, he said, "No, I am now well-informed on 6,000 ways you cannot do it."

When God created you and me, He made no mistake. Our job is to let a winner—Jesus—lead the way. Our failures can be merely stepping-stones to the future. "If God is for us, who can be against us?" (Rom. 8:31).

9. Dream a New Dream

As a result of my own brokenness, God brought a new dream into sharp focus. I was to pioneer a healing fellowship for the "unchurched thousands" where the broken could come and be healed, where the discouraged would come and be lifted, and where those searching for love would receive Christ's love. Out of what was once nothing but a mental picture, God raised up New Hope Community Church to heal thousands of hurting people all across Portland, Oregon.

God has done the same thing with countless other pastors and leaders. As they have dreamed a magnificent dream, God has used them to do something greater than they've ever done before.

As Dr. Schuller says in *Move Ahead with Possibility Thinking* (152):

> After the night comes a new day,
> After winter, a new spring,
> After the storm, a sun,
> After sin comes forgiveness,
> After defeat, another chance.

10. Turn Your Scars into Stars

When I laid on the beach in 1970, shouting at God through gut-wrenching pain, I had no idea He would enable me to start over again. But when I started New Hope Community Church, I was not alone. My beautiful wife and best friend, Margi, planted it with me and traveled every step of the 23-year journey there. We have continued the trek together these years since at Asbury Theological Seminary's Beeson Center. Out of terrible pain, He has brought great gain!

God's beauty from ashes is seen not only in my personal life but also in the ministry of New Hope itself. During our second year, for example, we received terrible news 11 days before Christmas. Without any advance warning and with no apparent reason, we were given notice by the management of the 82nd Drive-In Theater that our services would be terminated the following Sunday. The heartbreaking letter concluded, "It has been nice knowing you."

A person with hope cannot be defeated.

What a smashing blow! As I asked God what to do, He led me to design a walk-in service at a spacious indoor theater that would have cost $1 million if we had to build it ourselves. We began to plan ahead toward spring, when we would find a new outdoor theater. As it worked out, the 82nd Drive-In Theater was sold and the new management welcomed us back with open arms.

In the coming weeks and years, we moved ahead stronger than ever. By the time Margi and I accepted the call from the Beeson Center, our dream had been fulfilled; the church had 6,400 members. Eighty percent of these had never belonged to a church before.

My mentor Robert Schuller coined the expression "Turn your scars into stars," and it has become a source of inspiration to thousands of people, including myself. It has caused me to realize that with God, the best is always yet to come. Our hope in God kept us going and keeps me from being defeated to this day.

What matters to God is not where I have been, but where I am going. A person with hope cannot be defeated. The Christian full of hope knows that God will always bring something good out of bad. Truly "with God all things are possible" (Matt. 19:26).

WHY WE DON'T DELEGATE

Elton Trueblood, a lifetime advocate of lay ministry, said, "The laity are not the passengers of a ship. They are members of the crew." George Hunter's book *Church for the Unchurched* examines a number of today's breakthrough congregations. They cover a wide range of denominations and geographies. They differ in style, but they all value laypeople in ministry. In short, churches that make a difference find ways to release God's people to reach and serve other people in Jesus' name.

Why, then, do pastors tend to do the church's ministry all by themselves? What prevents them from sharing the privileges of ministry with God's people? Why do they, like Moses, need the "Jethro Principles" of delegation seen in Exod. 18:12-27?

Biggest Issue: Insecurities

Personal insecurity is probably the main obstacle to effective delegation. It took me until my mid-40s to stop comparing myself with others. Only then did I become comfortable with the person God made me to be.

If you don't grow secure enough in the Lord and in His love, you won't be free to let other people be themselves. You can't delight in others who are doing significant ministry if you're an insecure person. You won't trust them, and they won't be confident in stretching themselves.

I remember sitting in a men's gathering at New Hope Community Church as the pastor there. One of our young men was preaching, and the crowd was eating it up. Watching this young man connect so well with our men, I caught myself beginning to feel jealous. I was somewhat responsible for this dilemma because I had informally trained and coached this layman in how to speak to a crowd.

I sat there thinking, "Do I like the fact that everyone is enjoying him?" The decision: "Yes, he's one of my boys!" Effectively equipping the saints "for the work of the ministry" (Eph. 4:12, KJV) means that some of them will excel in areas beyond us. Maybe *many* of them will!

God wanted to mature me to where I enjoyed seeing other people's accomplishments. In time my biggest joy in ministry was enabling others to succeed. Whether it was leading someone to faith in Christ or visiting someone in the hospital, I began to genuinely enjoy seeing the people of the church outshine me. Today I get a bigger kick out of others who are effectively using their spiritual gifts than from my own achievements.

My vision for ministry must be bigger than my insecurities.

Wanting to Care for Everyone

A second obstacle to delegation is our own and others' expectations. In recent years I received a letter from a lady who said, "Twenty-five years ago my husband was in the hospital and you didn't come call on me. Please forgive me for being bitter toward you." She's typical of people who expect all the visitation to come from the pastor. I gave that level of care to a certain group in the church— my board, my staff, and my neighbors—because I needed to model ministry to teach it. However, I also had to limit my span of care; we can reach only so far. To reach farther, we must multiply our span of care through other people.

Some Christians (such as this woman who wrote me) will never be satisfied unless they receive personal attention from the pastor. But many others do not have those expectations. Still others could be taught not to have those expectations if they regularly receive a high quality of shepherdlike care through small groups.

As the number of trained lay pastors at New Hope Community Church grew, soon their reach was far beyond what I could personally do. At any waking hour of any day, one or more groups were meeting, offering care one to another in Jesus' name.

I could never be that available. If you have to do everything yourself, your ministry will not grow beyond the number of hands you can personally hold. My personal reach is tiny compared to all the needs that *could* be touched.

My vision for ministry had to be bigger than my personal desire to be the personal, pastoral caregiver for everyone.

Needing to Control Everything

I also had to give up controlling everything going on at the church. One day at New Hope I discovered three ministries I didn't know we had. Here I was—the founding pastor. How could anything happen without my blessing? My first reaction was indignance that I didn't personally know about these ministries. Then I decided that it was a pretty exciting situation when people felt free to put their ideas to work without having to ask my personal permission. My vision for ministry had to be bigger than my need for control.

Motivation for Delegation

What moves pastors to learn how to delegate? What motivates some is sheer desperation. They become so overwhelmed and fatigued that they begin allowing others to take on significant ministry responsibility. Gradually they come to see the joy others have in gift mobilization.

God has never given me a vision I could accomplish alone.

For me the motivation to delegate was to accomplish the vision and dream of our church. That was the driving force that kept me going. Without other people, I couldn't fulfill my calling to reach the unchurched thousands in Portland.

In fact, God has never given me a vision I could accomplish alone. Fulfillment of each vision has always required other people. Only what's shared multiplies. When the vision is bigger than anything that holds you back, it will drive you beyond your reluctance to delegate.

My biggest regret in 23 years of ministry in Portland is that we didn't do more. Some pastors want to make followers. I want to make leaders—to develop other people and release their giftedness. Look across your own church and ask if God would have you do likewise.

15

LOOKING OUT FOR MURPHY'S LAW

Each year another professor and I hopscotch the country, interviewing prospective students for the Beeson Pastor Program. We fly to one airport for a morning interview and then head to another city for an afternoon appointment.

One day the timing was particularly critical. As my colleague and I hastened to catch a connecting segment, we heard the dreaded news: "We're sorry to report that this flight has been canceled." We watched a man near us react by getting red in the face. He started swearing. His neck veins bulged. We thought he'd pop a blood vessel. A woman nearby screamed at the ticket agent, who of course could not override the decision to cancel our flight.

By contrast my colleague, Ellsworth Kalas, modeled the fruit of the Spirit. He looked at me, grinned, and said, "Murphy's Law, at work again!"

It doesn't matter who you are or where you live. In some way or another, you will encounter what seasoned air travelers experience every third or fourth trip. It's nicknamed Murphy's Law. This axiom proclaims that if anything can go wrong, it will. Murphy's-Law situations are beyond your control or ability to change.

When Murphy's Law strikes, you only have two choices. First, you can react negatively, trying to fight it. This strategy is like hitting your head against a stone wall. Second, you can face reality and respond positively. You can accept what you can't change and work creatively to find solutions.

Murphy's Law Is Impossible to Avoid

No amount of classroom preparation could ever prepare you for the realities of Murphy's Law at work in parish ministry. Yet everyday life in ministry is full of times when we least expect the worst (and we certainly don't want it), but nevertheless it hits us. Certainly in the apostle Paul's chronicle of imprisonments, shipwrecks, floggings, whippings, stonings, and numerous other life-endangering circumstances and pressures (see 2 Cor. 11:23-28), much could be described as Murphy's Law instances of the worst possible scenarios coming true.

Reality is that you can't pastor very long without being struck not once but again and again with Murphy's Law. Yet Paul didn't react negatively, become bitter, or give in to a victim mentality. Nor should we.

According to Paul, we are not perfect but are still in process. "Not that I . . . have already been made perfect, but I press on to take hold of that for which Christ Jesus took hold of me. . . . Forgetting what is behind and straining toward what is ahead" (Phil. 3:12-13). Why, then, should we expect everything in the church to be perfect and to work with perfection?

How to Make the Best of Murphy's Law

To be a great leader you have to live with one foot in reality—in the truth of everyday life as it is in the church. Meanwhile you place the other foot into the vision of where, with God's help, you're going to lead your people. That's how the apostle Paul kept pressing forward; that's how you and I can press forward too.

If you wait until everything is perfect to do something, you won't ever do anything.

We can take a lesson from how God made trees. If we don't flex and bend, we will break when the storm comes. At the same time, the tree has roots that hold it steady.

Here are ways some variations of Murphy's Law have shown up in the churches I've known or served as pastor:

1. About the time you get one area of ministry working really well, another ministry will fall into difficulties.

2. No matter how hard you work in casting a vision, some people won't get it. These individuals will leave your church for a variety of reasons you haven't even thought about. Their reasoning may even seem strange to you.

3. A lot of things that look good on paper and sound great in books don't work in the local parish. For example, *assigning* people to small groups looks good on paper, but when you try it the result is Murphy's Law. (People need to *choose* their group based on affinity and relationships.)

4. If you wait until everything is perfect to do something, you won't ever do anything. Nothing is ever perfect or completely finished in church work. You're always in process. So are the people and their ministries. Things are always in a state of flux and change.

5. If a great baseball player can bat .350, he can still win the batting championship. Nobody bats a thousand. Similarly, you can be a champion leader as a pastor if you keep making "hits" in your prayerful decision making. Everything you do doesn't have to be a grand slam, a home run, or even a constant hit.

Maybe Murphy Was an Optimist

I began this chapter with an airline story. Have you ever been in an airport that wasn't under construction? Where growth or new opportunity is present, you'll usually find construction underway, along with its accompanying challenges to the people using the facility.

Likewise, I have yet to be in a cutting-edge church that wasn't still "under construction." And yes, in churches like that Murphy's Law also shows up during the process, right on cue. They are not exempt.

How to Be a Victor Instead of a Victim When Murphy's Law Strikes

1. Remember who called you. God is bigger than what is wrong.
2. Keep focused on the vision God has given you.
3. Keep the main thing the main thing.
4. Be a problem solver and not a part of the problem.
5. Use failure as stepping-stones to future success.
6. Remember, it's always the darkest before the morning; never give up hope.
7. Do what you can with what you have where you are, remembering the promise that God will give the increase (see 1 Cor. 3:6).
8. Make up your mind that no matter what happens you will be a lover of people. Love people regardless of how they treat you. You will always win with love.

If even the gates of hell cannot prevail against the expansion of the church, then Murphy's Law need not cause any more emotion than Dr. Kalas's grinning comment of "Murphy's Law, at work again!" By the way, we rescheduled the interview and flew out the next morning.

LIGHTENING YOUR LOAD BY SHARING RESPONSIBILITY

T hat's good advice," my insightful wife commented as I put down the phone. "But that's not what you did when *you* were the pastor."

She was right. I had been honored by a call from Ray Cotton, the able leader who followed me as senior pastor at New Hope Community Church. After he asked my opinion, I had said, "Ray, my friend, don't bear this burden by yourself. Don't take all the responsibility. This isn't your problem alone. Get together the key board leaders and staff pastors, share the matter with them, and become responsible together for how you'll solve it."

During four pastorates spanning three decades, I struggled under some loads I could have lightened by sharing responsibility with others. Whenever a problem arose, too often I felt as if it was my job alone to come up with a solution. That put unnecessary overloads of stress on myself. As Margi's comment indicated, I could have let others walk with me. I am still learning how to lighten my load by sharing responsibility with others.

In order to advance a church and to grow personally as a leader, a pastor needs to learn what to be responsible for—and what *not* to take full responsibility for! To be a maturing pastor of a changing church, you must continually work at helping laypeople develop a greater sense of ownership. If the church is having trouble with growing, maybe the pastor is not sharing responsibility the right way. This chapter will help you sort through the important issues at hand.

Early Habits

When you start out planting or leading a smaller church, you tend to take responsibility for everything that takes place. If you are not personally accountable, chances are the event or emphasis doesn't happen!

How long should you follow that approach? When should you begin to share ownership with others?

As I often tell the Beeson pastor group I train: "Before you can grow to the next level of ministry, you will have to change." Change never comes easily, but not changing is even more painful in the long run.

The sooner you learn to share ministry with others, as Jethro instructed Moses, the sooner Jethro's advice will become a reality to you: This strategy will "make your load lighter, because they will *share* it with you" (Exod. 18:22, emphasis added).

If you're responsible for the same things in a larger church as you were in the smaller church, the load will be too heavy for you. Pastors, especially founding ones, often carry an overload of ownership. The common pitfall of church planters is that they think they should continue to operate the same way they did in the early days.

In the early days at New Hope, when we received notice that we couldn't meet at our worship location anymore, I took sole responsibility to find a new place to meet. If we needed a certain amount of money to underwrite the next step in our growth, I took responsibility for it.

When we became a church of 6,000 members and the business manager called saying we needed, for example $50,000 within 24 hours, I would personally take responsibility instead of getting our Finance Committee together and asking how we as a team should handle it.

I'm one of many pastors who should have begun sharing responsibility much sooner. I was like an engine that didn't know how to shift gears. Constantly running at a high RPM overworks an engine and wears it out. By comparison, a pastor will last longer by figuring out and using the right gear ratio!

First Steps

For what should the pastor alone be responsible? Which responsibilities need to be shared with others? The answers vary according to the leader's maturity and the church's growth stage. If the church is growing, the answer is often in constant transition.

However, pastoral care is one essential area to share as quickly as possible. Many first-time pastors start out being the caregiver who responds, in solo fashion, to everyone who calls.

If that is your ministry model, you may be doing more chaplaincy than leadership development. Can you take someone along with you on your next hospital visit, prospect call, and discipleship meeting? It's vitally important that you train others (see 2 Tim. 2:2) and that you equip the saints for the work of ministry (see Eph. 4:11-12).

Better, can you follow Jesus' example with His apostles and send your people out for ministry—without you? (see Matt. 10). In that way, you're letting the church be the church. Equip them, encourage them, coach them, and listen to their reports when they come back from ministry.

As the church increases its scope of ministry, you can begin scheduling designated times for meeting with people. Can you recruit an administrative assistant who will calendar people for appointments at your time and your place?

This discipline affirms that you have other responsibilities as well. Big changes occur when you no longer build your schedule around responding immediately to everyone who calls. This practice not only saves your time but also guards you emotionally. The transition process begins when you intentionally start sharing the responsibility for pastoral care with others.

The key is having a secretary or administrative assistant who asks and discerns: "Is this an emergency or will it wait a few days?" Most situations that wait a few days or more will cancel out because people will have already taken care of the need.

When I pastored New Hope, I met on Fridays with anyone who had called and made this kind of appointment through my well-trained assistant. Using this schedule anyone could have access to me, but I wasn't burning up all my emotional energies by overloading on daily emergencies.

More Responsibilities You Can Share

Here are some guidelines that have helped me learn which responsibilities to keep and which to share:

Leaders who are growing take responsibility for the vision and direction of the church.

---

1. I'm not responsible for the attitudes and actions of anyone but myself. I can do something about my own perspectives and responses. When my own house is in order, I can be right with God and at peace with others. However, I'm not responsible for others' choices to attack me or behave in an un-Christlike manner.

2. I am responsible for the stewardship of my own life. If I am feeling overwhelmed, I have no one to blame but myself. Likewise, if you're bleeding to death from an overload of responsibility, you can't help anyone else. If you don't take care of yourself, no one else will. (So take responsibility to take care of yourself!)

3. I'm not responsible for others' personal obligations. Every church will have "user types" who want to hold their pastor or counselor responsible because they don't have a job or didn't pay their rent. We should respond compassionately to human need, but we needn't bear the level of burden that tries to make up for where an individual needed to take personal responsibility.

4. I must always be responsible to model ministry with a few while teaching others to deal with the larger numbers.

5. I can never give up being responsible for setting the sail, casting the vision, and being the spiritual leader of the church I've been called of God to shepherd. Leaders who are growing take responsibility for the vision and direction of the church. Neither can we give up personal responsibility to win people to Christ and to care for others. We simply expand those ministry privileges through other people.

6. The other extreme is the person who takes responsibility for nothing. I always need to be responsible when something goes wrong. Don't play a blame game. Just accept responsibility and move on.

People Appreciate Being Involved

It's fun to watch our Beeson pastors go back into full-time ministry after their year of intensive study. One of my doctor of ministry students, Denny Heiberg, had taken a one-year leave from his congregation. Before his academic year with me was complete, he went back to his pulpit to preach on Easter Sunday. The next evening he gathered a couple dozen key leaders to praise them for how well they had stepped up to the plate and taken leadership responsibilities during his absence.

"Do you want me to come back with a renewed direction for the church all mapped out?" he asked them. "Or do you want to help develop it?"

"We want to own it," they replied. "You frame it but let us help shape it."

"I'm not the same person I was when I left 10 months ago!" he warned, probing them for openness to possible changes.

"We're not the same either!" they agreed. "You used to be the hitter, catcher, outfielder, and base runner for us. When you come back, we want you to be the coach. We want to be the team."

In short, the growing leader must be a continual learner in the area of releasing ministry to others. That's what the word *disciple* implies. You don't do yourself any good—or prolong your ministry—if you don't learn how to share responsibility as your church develops.

Grave Consequences If You Don't Share

As you grow a church, the natural progression is to take on more and more responsibility, eventually reaching a point that could break your back. Mistakenly, I thought for years that as a leader I should be able to carry anything. I have learned that everyone can carry only so much—and for a limited time.

My friend Jim Garlow, senior pastor of Skyline Wesleyan Church just outside San Diego, found himself carrying an overwhelming load. He had hit the ground running when he became pastor in 1995. The church had fought all kinds of zoning battles in a 10-year effort to relocate to more adequate facilities. They had dealt with complicated, expensive environmental problems. They had spent over $7 million and still not one shovelful of dirt had been turned. They had been through three demanding financial campaigns.

Now came news that they needed to qualify for an $8.5 million loan, sell their "tired" old campus for $3 million, and pledge nearly $8 million more. Financial consultants said this was impossible. The people were discouraged. Jim knew he was facing a make-or-break turning point, yet he secretly feared the building campaign might drown him. In addition he was feeling overcome by the $62,500 weekly operating budget. As a result, he was not sleeping at nights.

As he prayed and as people prayed for him, Jim got an idea. He called together 250 of the church's top givers for a special meeting. He explained how he couldn't sleep at night because of the huge weight he felt.

He symbolized his concern by trying to lift a 250-pound set of barbells. He couldn't manage them without hurting himself.

Then he pointed out that under everyone's chair was a 1-pound weight. He asked each person to join him in lifting the weights. Now 250 pounds were lifted together.

The illustration made a powerful point: When a load is shared, it's not too heavy for anyone. By distributing the responsibility, Jim found an emotional release that allowed him to sleep at night. This well-being in turn made possible fresh creativity to lead people into the new financial campaign.

Later, when Jim issued the call for additional finances, a miracle occurred beyond what any financial planners said would happen. God did the impossible and raised the needed prompted pledges of nearly $8 million through the congregation. Everybody benefited, and Jim lived to give testimony about it!

What would have happened if Jim had not shared this responsibility? The results would have been quite different.

Never-Ending Process

"To whom much is given, much is required," Jesus said. We must maximize what God has given us. That involves learning how to maximize time, to develop others, to help others take ownership, and to share responsibility so that we can last longer. Being a good steward means learning when and how to bring others to a greater level of participation in the concerns I'm carrying.

Why not lighten your own load by sharing more responsibility with others? Keep asking yourself, "What am I carrying that I need to shoulder with others?"

This is not a selfish request

> Where is your load of responsibility too heavy? Where do you need to invite others to share the burden with you?
> 1. Needed changes in the church
> 2. Financial matters
> 3. Pastoral care
> 4. Leadership development
> 5. Conflict resolution
> 6. Property purchases and building projects
> 7. Launching new programs
> 8. Missions and outreach
> 9. Staffing and personnel decisions

for you. It's the lifeblood of what empowered ministry and biblical community are about. Your health and well being may depend upon these changes.

17

MULTIPLYING YOUR MOST LIMITED RESOURCE

Do you ever wish you could clone yourself to get more done? Have you ever felt you have too much to do in too little time? Stress doctors teach that we are most likely to feel overpressured when the demands are greater than our resources. The usual pinch point is time. That's your greatest physical resource.

The hardest person for a leader to manage is himself or herself, and the most challenging dimension of self-management involves time. Effective leaders must do more than set the right priorities for themselves. They must also gain skill at multiplying their time.

Leaders who learn how to do more things in less time know how to multiply themselves. They leverage their time to make the greatest impact on the most people.

I first began learning this lesson when I was in my 30s, working long days, joyfully giving most of my waking-hour energies in service to Christ. One of my mentors, a Nazarene pastor named Les Parrott II, suggested that I multiply my efforts rather than my hours. He helped me see how much sense it makes to work smarter rather than harder and longer.

Multiplying Your Resources

"If you're going to pour yourself into developing good sermons," he asked, "why not get more mileage out of them?" Over time, here is what I began to do with the typed messages:

- Made them available for people to take home and reread or give to friends.
- Mailed them to members who were absent or to recent guests.
- Built them into books as chapters or major sections.
- Excerpted them in church newsletters and training manuals.
- Summarized them in outlines and discussion questions for home-based care groups to use.
- Developed radio and television programs from the same material.

As cassette technology came of age, we made sermon copies for members, shut-ins, guests, young people away at college or in the military, and any number of outreach contexts. In fact a good book, *The Comprehensive Guide to Cassette Ministry* by Johnny Berguson with Warren Bird, gives almost 100 different examples of how to multiply the impact of a pastor's sermons through audiocassettes.

Multiply Your Services

You can also leverage time better in the use of your church facilities. Today's church plants and church relocations frequently construct multipurpose buildings first. Then they build sanctuaries or worship centers. Why? With a single building campaign, you can house worship services *and* fellowship dinners *and* numerous other large-group activities. One facility houses multiple functions.

In the same way, why not multiply your preparation hours by adding a worship service? More people will be touched when you have multiple services, all for roughly the same planning time on your part.

People like choices. Studies show that 8 out of 10 churches that begin an additional worship service will experience a measurable increase in the total number of worshipers, the finances given by those worshipers, and the number of lives changed through a relationship with Jesus Christ.

Church authority Lyle Schaller suggests that half of all churches in America should add a new service to their weekend offerings. Researcher W. Charles Arn says, "It's encouraging to hear of the number of churches that already have more than one service and are still seeking to add an additional one."

Arn's writings suggest eight doable action points:

Step 1. Identify and describe your target audience.

Step 2. Agree on the purpose/goal of the new service.

Step 3. Identify the relevant issues and themes to which the service can speak.

Step 4. Design the service(s).

Step 5. Determine the time and place to meet.

Step 6. Communicate with your target audience.

Step 7. Follow up on the visitors and prospects.

Step 8. Evaluate the service.

Making a 9- to 15-month investment—the time typically needed from first introducing the idea through postlaunch evaluation—will double or triple the number of people to whom you minister with the time you put into message preparation for years to come. Or if you're like my friend Steve Sjogren at Vineyard Community Church, Cincinnati, Ohio, you'll multiply the number of people *many* times over. At one point the church ran seven services and was praying about adding an eighth!

The most common objection to multiple services is what I call the "village church" idea. It's the misguided notion that the entire congregation needs to gather as one big group every week. Can you ever get all your people together at one time? You can't. No matter what day or time you announce, one person's work schedule will be at odds and another person's children will have a soccer tournament.

Jesus said to be fruitful, not just faithful (see Matt. 7:16-20; John 15:1-16). Churches must move into multiplication mode. That's the only way to meet with your church's entire constituency, much less do maximum outreach.

Multiply Your Leadership Network

The more lay pastors New Hope Community Church developed, the more nurture and love multiplied. Our care groups met at different times and at various places. Meetings convened from morning to night: from a 6 A.M. men's meeting; through daytime groups for retirees, businesspeople, and stay-at-home moms; to evening groups involving different life stages. Groups convened in restaurants, office lunchrooms, college dormitories, apartments, and homes.

Build leaders, and they'll build ministries.

I could never give that amount or level of care, even if I were personally available 24 hours a day, seven days a week. New Hope's network of care emerged only as I multiplied myself through others. As church consultant Carl George says in *How to Break Growth Barriers*, the change needed is from personal shepherd of each sheep to "the dispenser of shepherd's crooks" (93). Then out of those people you create leaders who, in turn, create the next generation of groups.

In 1972 (before New Hope began celebration services on Sundays) my wife and I formed and led a Tender Loving Care group. Out of that we created the next groups, and out of those came leaders for many other groups. Four of New Hope's staff pastors today emerged from those first groups. Their first ministry had been to lead a small group.

We eventually saw the day when 500 trained lay pastors provided effective pastoral care to more than 5,000 people. This is multiplication of my pastoral care through others! Our underlying strategy: Build leaders, and they'll build ministries.

Multiply Your Dependence on God

Many years ago I heard Chicago insurance multimillionaire W. Clement Stone speak at the Robert H. Schuller Institute for Successful Church Leadership. He concluded his message by saying, "Think, think, think, think, think, think, think, think." Then he left the room!

His message caused me to start thinking more about *what* I was doing, *why*, and *how* I could be more effective. As I meditated on such scriptures as Jesus' miracle with the loaves and fishes, I realized that it's not more time I need, but heavenly wisdom and skill in multiplying the time I already have.

Phoenix First Assembly of God's Tommy Barnett predicts in his book *Multiplication*, "Purpose-driven people, filled by the Spirit with visionary dreams and praying for His power, will multiply the church in this generation." It's time to unlock those biblical factors to multiply your effectiveness in leadership and ministry, to the glory of Christ and the expansion of His Church.

In total dependence on God, you can learn how to multiply your resources, your people, and your leaders.

Effective Leaders Think Regularly About Reaching More People by Multiplying Their

- Building(s) and equipment
- Choirs, worship team(s), and number of services
- Sermon preparation efforts
- Pastoral care through developing more small groups
- Lay leaders and potential lay leaders
- Outreach opportunities through need-meeting ministries
- Skills in delegation, empowerment, and permission-giving

SECTION FOUR

Break Free from the Prisons of "Problem People"

18

COPING WITH DIFFICULT PEOPLE

To be an effective church leader, you must work with many kinds of people. This includes "irregular" people. Some of the finest Christian leaders I know have trouble getting along with difficult persons.

"Extra care required" individuals consistently act sneaky, hostile, negative, or unresponsive to others' needs. These men and women cause all varieties of relationship problems. Normal communication fails to get through.

The Bible says, "If it is possible, as far as it depends on you, live at peace with everyone" (Rom. 12:18). This principle applies to leaders as well; we need to do our best at getting along with everyone. Here are eight strategies for success when dealing with difficult people.

Type 1: The Sherman Tank

According to Robert M. Bramson in *Coping with Difficult People*, the Sherman tank image describes the aggressive, often hostile person who tries to roll over others. This pushy, manipulating individual may victimize you and then turn around and make you feel like a crook.

How do you handle a Sherman tank? You don't have to fight, but you do need to decide, "I am not going to allow this person to run over me." You must stand up for yourself in a Christlike way.

A businessman, convicted of cheating on several hundred thousand dollars' worth of taxes, was sent to prison. During the trial and incarceration, his church stood by him as much as possible.

His sentence included making restitution for the money he had stolen. Upon his release, he tried to steamroll his pastor and church administrator into paying his debt for him. "There we were, listening to the man who had committed the crime and feeling as if we were the criminals," the business administrator later commented.

They told the man in no uncertain terms that the church was not responsible for his sin. Once confronted by the straightforward truth, the manipulation game ended. This Sherman tank respected leaders who had the courage and audacity to stand up to him.

Type 2: The Space Cadet

A space cadet acts and thinks as if he or she came from a different planet. Unable to listen to others, this difficult person lives in a self-created world.

A missionary was captured by cannibals and thrown into a cooking pot. Certain his last hour had come, he was surprised to see the chief sink to his knees and lift his hands in prayer.

"Am I to understand you are a practicing Christian?" the missionary called out hopefully.

"I certainly am," replied the cannibal chief, "but please don't interrupt me when I'm saying grace."

Some people, both Christians and non-Christians, operate on a wavelength different from those around them. They park where they're not supposed to. They show up where they don't belong. They take charge when someone else has been designated to lead. If you expect emotional responsiveness from these persons, you will probably be hurt because you are not going to receive it.

The best way to get along with space cadets is to make up your mind not to let them drive you bonkers. To accept a person as being from a different planet means recognizing that he or she is probably not going to change. Ultimately, you are not responsible for another's actions and attitudes. As authors Henry Cloud and John Townsend say in *The Mom Factor*, "Codependency is basically a boundaries problem. If you are codependent, you don't allow the ones you love to be responsible for their own problems."

Type 3: The Volcano

Difficult people of the volcano type are either exploding or building up steam to prepare for the next explosion. People who live with them walk around on pins and needles, never knowing when another eruption is coming.

Volcanoes often get their way by intimidating others. Wherever they are, they generate tension.

Tom Peterson is a respected businessman at a church I pastored. One day I asked him what he does with a guy who buys a new color television set to watch the Super Bowl, only to return the next day like a raging bull because the set went on the blink in the middle of the game.

"I stand there and listen," Tom told me. "I listen for a long time without saying a word, except to agree with what the person is saying. I give him time to run down. When he has gotten his story pretty well out, I ask him to tell it one more time, so I am sure I understand what happened. The next time, though, he usually talks in normal voice tones."

Tom demonstrates an effective way of handling a volcano. He listens empathetically and answers gently. Prov. 15:1 also summarizes this strategy: "A gentle answer turns away wrath, but a harsh word stirs up anger."

Type 4: The Spoiler

This person complains chronically. No matter what happens, the spoiler grumbles and acts negatively. For example, a woman griped because she lived in a small, rented apartment. Now she lives in a luxurious, 10-room house in one of the finest sections of the city, but she's still complaining. If you asked her to write down all her objections, and then you proceeded to eliminate every one, she would simply develop a new list of complaints.

You cannot satisfy spoilers because they never feel satisfied with themselves. No matter what you do, they won't be pleased.

Pick out any successful ministry where people are won to Jesus, lives are healed, and relationships are put back together through the power of God. Inside every one you will find some spoiler types. Thousands of people are receiving help, but all the spoiler sees is the negative.

What, then, is a good strategy for dealing with a spoiler? Recognize this difficult person for being a model of negative thinking that you do not want to adopt. Instead, choose and cultivate your own positive mental attitude. As the Bible teaches, "Fix your thoughts on what is true and good and right. Think about things that are pure and lovely, and dwell on the fine, good things in others. Think about all you can praise God for and be glad about" (Phil. 4:8, TLB).

Type 5: The Wet Blanket

No matter what is proposed, the wet blanket automatically responds, "It can't be done," "It won't work," "It's never been done before," or "It's impossible." This difficult person is the classic impossibility thinker.

I had a friend who counseled a wet blanket. She was unmotivated to find a job and get off welfare. He spent hundreds of hours trying to help her do something for herself. He once gave her a list of 25 things she could do to improve her miserable state in life. She responded by shooting down every possibility.

How do you get along with a wet blanket? Allow this person the right to be sour and pessimistic. But don't allow that attitude to dampen *your* enthusiasm for life. Don't surrender your leadership; continue to be a possibility thinker. Remember, "with God all things are possible" (Matt. 19:26) and "For all the promises of God in Him are Yes, and in Him Amen, to the glory of God through us" (2 Cor. 1:20, NKJV).

Type 6: The Garbage Collector

Garbage collectors love to rehearse and replay the injuries they have suffered at the hands of other people. They nurse their wounds and hold onto their wounded spirits. They fixate on negative emotions. Like spreading manure around, they stink up everything.

These persons maintain a cover, often thin and transparent, from behind which they take potshots like a sniper. "Their weapons are rocks hidden in snowballs: innuendoes, *sotto voce* remarks, not-too-subtle digs, non-playful teasing, and the like," says Bramson in *Coping with Difficult People* (1988).

Managing Your Time with Difficult People

Sometimes pastors feel so enmeshed with needy or irregular people in their congregations that they can't free up time to multiply themselves. Here are some tips on how to counterattack with positive actions. They are each stated in the spirit of Heb. 12:14: "Make every effort to live in peace with all men."

1. Be Confident in Who You Are. When relating to a difficult person, remember that your self-worth does not depend on that person's opinion of you.

2. Don't Allow Yourself to Overreact. Even the most difficult person usually has some good attributes and behaviors. It's important to see these as well.

3. Refuse to Play the Difficult Person's Games. Learn to say no when difficult people try to manipulate or gain control over you, or they will consume an enormous amount of your time and energy.

4. When You Need to Confront, Do So Immediately. The sooner you stand up to a difficult person, the better off you will be. Each day you wait allows more control and damage by the person's destructive misbehavior.

5. Have Realistic Expectations. People who are hurt can't give much love. Save yourself a lot of pain and rejection by not expecting a difficult person to give you what you need.

6. Stop Trying to Change the Difficult Person in Your Life. Do not try to change anyone who does not want to change. Sometimes you must stop taking responsibility for someone else's bad habits.

7. Keep Yourself from Becoming the Difficult Person's Slave. In trying to relate to someone who is verbally abusive or manipulative, remember that you always have a choice to say no.

8. Let God Lead You Through Your Struggle with That Difficult Person. Do not be robbed of your inner peace. Every time we turn our eyes on Jesus and ask for His help, His peace comes into our hearts (see Phil. 4:7).

Garbage collectors are basically too cowardly to follow through on their feelings. They need your prayers. Sometimes they will respond to your attempts to be God's servant in bringing the healing and change they need.

If their behavior continues in a disruptive manner that harms other people, you may need to confront them in front of other mature people. Ask direct questions and hold them to an answer: "Is this how you feel?" "Is this what you'd like to say?" "Do you believe this, or don't you?" Pin them down and do not let them squirm out of taking responsibility for their emotions.

As with the spoiler and the wet blanket, do not allow the garbage collector's ill feelings to restrict your attitude and outlook.

Type 7: The User

Users include alcoholics, drug addicts, compulsive gamblers, emotionally dependent adults, and spoiled children. They will do anything to manipulate you into providing *what* they want *when* they want it. If you're not careful, they will make you their slave.

I'll never forget my first pastoral-ministry experience with a user. I think the previous pastor moved to another church just to get away from her. I hadn't been in town a week when she began phoning me every day, talking for two or three hours. I quickly discovered that she had no interest in growing or changing. She only wanted to use me for her daily emotional dumping ground.

In the process, she depleted all my emotional energy. I had nothing left to give to the many other people in the congregation.

After a month, I got smart and set some boundaries. I said, "I'm concerned about you, and I want to help, but here are the limits. You may call me every Friday morning at 9:30, and we will talk for 15 minutes."

You can get along with a user by applying this same tough-love principle. Sometimes the only way to get along with a user is to set limits that keep you from being used and abused.

Type 8: The Emotionally Handicapped

Some people have been so deeply wounded emotionally that they have developed a handicap when it comes to relating to others. You may show love and kindness, which they may simply ignore. Or they may go to the other extreme and attack you. Often the emotionally handicapped are simply good people who have been battered and scarred emotionally.

Let God's love and wisdom be yours as you develop successful strategies for dealing with the irregular persons in your parish.

In many cases your biggest challenge will be to look beyond their unsatisfying behaviors, see the pain in their eyes, and sense the woundedness in their spirits. They need healing. Jesus calls us to be His agents one to another. As Scripture says, "Pray for each other so that you may be healed" (James 5:16).

Like the good Samaritan, you need to be compassionate and loving to those who have been abused and victimized. The good Samaritan contributed to a miracle of healing by picking up his wounded "neighbor" and caring for him (Luke 10:25-37).

By identifying the areas of need in the difficult people you serve, you can respond in ways that lead toward wholeness and maturity—for you and for them. Let God's love and wisdom be yours as you develop successful strategies for dealing with the irregular persons in your parish.

19

HANDLING OPPOSITION IN A POSITIVE WAY

Dwight Eisenhower summarized his military experience by saying, "There are no victories at bargain prices." In ministry, there is likewise a price to be paid. The bigger your vision, the bigger the price. Jesus said, "In this world you will have trouble. But take heart! I have overcome the world" (John 16:33).

This chapter will help you learn to handle opposition more effectively. First we'll look at outward forces that oppose us. Then we'll examine inward discouragement. Nehemiah, one of my favorite characters in the entire Bible, will be the role model for what we learn.

Be Willing to Be Broken

What breaks your heart? Do you look at your community and city and see the loneliness, the opposition to God, the fragmentation of people's lives—their pain, the broken families? Do those realities stir you inside? Do they drive you to your knees?

When Nehemiah heard the full extent of the shameful condition the city was in, he poured tears out of his heart for the people. "When I heard these things, I sat down and wept. For some days I mourned and fasted and prayed before the God of heaven" (Neh. 1:4).

Despite the fact that the returned exiles had been in Jerusalem for years, the walls of the city remained unrepaired, leaving its people defenseless and vulnerable. The rubble was stacked high everywhere. No one there believed anything could be done about the fallen wall. It was a disgrace to their natural pride. It showed how beaten they were as a people. Corporate self-esteem was at its lowest point.

The lesson here is that in service to God, only broken hearts will do. Think about a church you admire, one that seems to have it all together. If we could pull back the curtain and see the opposition—the hard places, setbacks, and tears —this church has undoubtedly faced over the years, only then would we begin to understand how God molded them to where they are today.

Some of you minister in places where the walls have broken down, the people are discouraged, and the rubble is high. God always brings in a leader who will let his or her heart be broken and who will go before the Lord. As God begins His work through that person, His purpose is made clear—transforming the people via a vision that leads them out of their "rubble" of discouragement and failure, and that brings them a new victory.

Expect Outward Opposition

Face reality: Every leader gets hit with criticism. If you have any amount of vision, you'll face obstacles and opposition rather quickly. Anything worthwhile requires God's help to make it through.

When Nehemiah began to rebuild the wall, the future seemed bright. "'Come let us rebuild the wall of Jerusalem, and we will no longer be in disgrace.' . . . They replied, 'Let us start rebuilding.' So they began this good work" (Neh. 2:17-18).

Yet two chapters later, the criticisms had begun. Leaders need to learn to expect opposition.

I'll never forget the journey when we were ready to buy our first piece of property for New Hope Community Church. I had walked the land with a couple of our leaders, and I had seen a dove at the top of a tree. So I called the proposed site the Promised Land. We raised the down payment—a miracle in itself—bought the land, and were convinced God wanted us to build our facilities upon it for His glory.

Then we went to get our zoning approvals. I received the biggest shock of my life. I thought everyone loved churches. Yet here were all these people organized to oppose us. The board turned us down, saying that we would put too much traffic on their road. We couldn't figure out what was going on, so we took it to court. It failed. We brought it back to the zoning board, and it failed again. (At that point, a friend said to me, "That was not a dove you saw in the tree, but a pigeon.)

We sold the land for a higher price than we paid for it. That gave us enough down payment for another piece of property, a lush green hillside along the interstate where the church facilities are located today.

For about three years we didn't know where God was in this property deal. After we got through the criticism, eventually it all made sense. We learned to expect opposition; every leader gets hit with criticism.

Refuse to Surrender to Negative People

Nehemiah got hit by the same kinds of opposition that church leaders face today.

Ridicule. Sanballat made fun of Nehemiah and the workers. "He became angry and was greatly incensed. He ridiculed the Jews" (Neh. 4:1). Ridicule can be contagious. People who are cowards will join in if someone takes the lead. In this case, Sanballat's associate, "Tobiah the Ammonite, who was at his side, said,

'What they are building—if even a fox climbed up on it, he would break down their wall of stones!'" (v. 3).

Resistance. Nehemiah reports that "they all plotted together to come and fight against Jerusalem and stir up trouble against it" (v. 8). To me one of the wonders of the world is how negative people in a church find each other and create a negative force. By some miracle, their negativity draws them together. The greater you're trying to do things for God to reach people, the more kinds of resistance you're going to experience.

Rumors. Nehemiah's opponents also fed on the people's fears by spreading rumors. "Also our enemies said, 'Before they know it or see us, we will be right there among them and will kill them and put an end to the work'" (v. 11).

As today, in Nehemiah's time the rumors were spread by those closest to the enemy, in his case "the Jews who lived near them" (v. 12). The Jews outside the city of Jerusalem, who lived near the enemy, were the ones most negative. What happens when you are around negative people all of the time? You become negative.

Also as today, in Nehemiah's time rumors become exaggerated as they are repeated. They "came and told us ten times over" (v. 12). Leaders don't swallow rumors. They expose rumors by proclaiming the truth.

Do these tactics of opposition show up in your congregation? If in doubt, think about the last time you listened to an earful and then replied, "Who told you that?" only to hear, "Well, I can't tell you."

The more quickly I can do something positive toward someone who has been negative toward me, the freer I become.

Whatever you do, don't surrender your leadership to negative people. When confronted with skunks, don't squeeze them at the wrong time or in the wrong place.

A funny thing happened in Darlington, Maryland, several years ago. A woman named Edith was coming home from a neighbor's house one Saturday afternoon. As she walked into the house, she saw five of her youngest children huddled together, concentrating with intense interest on something. She slipped near them, trying to discover the center of attention. What she saw amazed her. In the middle of the circle were several baby skunks. She screamed at the top of her voice, "Children, run!" In response, each kid grabbed a skunk, squeezed it tight, and ran!

There will be times in your ministry when someone is so negative that you'll have to remember: don't get in a fight with a skunk.

My father was a district superintendent for 29 years in the Nazarene Church in Central Ohio. He had a particular pastor on his district who ridiculed him, organized resistance to his leadership, and spread rumors. One day I asked my dad if he knew about it. He indicated that he did. I asked him why he didn't do something about it. I'll always remember his reply, "I'm not going to stoop to that level." Later I saw my dad stick up for this man and help him get placed in another church in spite of the fact that this negative man had predictably been very unsuccessful in other churches.

One of Dad's watchwords was the Golden Rule: "Always treat other people how you'd like to be treated" (see Matt. 7:12). From that wonderful heritage I learned always to act in love, no matter what other people do. I won't surrender who I am as a leader or a person to negative forces that come against me. I am responsible to God for my own actions and attitudes, and when I focus on that, it's amazing how God brings me through. That's what Paul meant when he said, "Overcome evil with good" (Rom. 12:21).

While I won't do things to boost negative people, such as putting them in leadership roles, I do go out of my way to show kindness. In fact, the more quickly I can do something positive toward someone who has been negative toward me, the freer I become. It's very important to pay attention to my spirit and to keep it whole inside.

Don't Expect an Easy Way Out

Great churches are built only with sweat, blood, and tears. If an easy way existed to grow a strong church, I would have found it, for I've looked for it all my life.

The door of success in ministry swings on the hinges of opposition. It is impossible to be a visionary leader in a church and to escape opposition.

Don't be surprised when you regularly receive criticism. I never lead a pastors' gathering without discovering at least one thing we all have in common: Someone left the church in the last month and faults the pastor for what happened.

In every setback you will find an opportunity for you as a leader. If you want to do everything you can to be effective where God has called you, then don't be surprised if God honors that desire. You're surrounded by people who need Jesus, and if you do what you can with what you have where God has called you, God will bless that.

Discouragement Is like Termite Damage

"I have failed here . . . and here . . . and here . . . and here, but that does not mean I'm a failure. It simply means I've not yet succeeded. A person may have many failings and yet be very far from being a failure. If I walk in God's way and draw on God's power, 'I can do all things through Christ who strengthens me'" (Phil. 4:13, NKJV).

The real battles of ministry are won or lost in your own inner spirit. When you are working hard and are constantly encountering opposition, you are going to become discouraged. Accept the facts: Opposition can wear down your spirit, opening you up to the termites of discouragement that eat away at your soul.

When is discouragement most likely to occur? For Nehemiah it came at the halfway mark, when they had "rebuilt the wall till all of it reached half its height" (Neh. 4:6). When you are worn out physically and overtaxed emotionally, you are more open to discouragement. At that point four "termites" of despair began gnawing at Nehemiah's spirit, according to verses 10-11: (1) Fatigue—"The strength of the laborers is giving out"; (2) Frustration—"So much rubble;" (3) Failure—"We cannot rebuild"; (4) Fear—"Enemies . . . will kill [us]."

In today's era of high-visibility megachurches, it's easy to mistakenly think that everything attempted by certain churches becomes a great success. That assumption would be a big mistake. Every pacesetting church, large and small, has a behind-the-scenes story that goes like this: "We tried this and it failed. We tried that and it failed. We tried again and failed again. We had to deal with discouragement. Finally, after learning from those experiences, we found God's breakthrough. Thank God we didn't give up."

Rely on God

Nehemiah's response to discouragement began with prayer: "Hear us, O our God, for we are despised" (Neh. 4:4). What a wonderful thing it is to talk to God about your critics and to cry out all of your pent-up feelings.

The greater the opposition, the more you need to rely on God in prayer. When you are discouraged, don't take it out on people; talk it out with God.

Sometimes you need to get away and rest. Sometimes you need quiet renewal with the Lord to renew your strength. Isa. 40:29 promises, "He gives strength to the weary and increases the power of the weak." Verse 31 continues, "They that wait upon the LORD shall renew their strength" (KJV).

Times of discouragement teach us how to overcome our fears with new faith in Christ. Someone has said, "Look at the world and be distressed; look within and be depressed; look at Christ and be at rest."

In Christ we don't have to surrender to our problems. We can find God's help to stick with the stuff and overcome opposition.

Christian philosopher Søren Kierkegaard said that you live life forward and you understand it backward. As I reflect on all the opposition I encountered over three decades of pastoral ministry, I see that the breakthroughs happened not by my own power or strength but by the Holy Spirit working in my life.

Respect the Opposition

Nehemiah's response showed his respect for the opposition. Up to this time, Nehemiah had been doing the praying. Now all the people joined him. "But we prayed to our God and posted a guard day and night to meet this threat" (Neh. 4:9). They got this idea by watching their leaders. Leaders lead by showing, not by telling.

Not only did they pray, but they also set a 24-hour watch "behind the lowest points of the wall at the exposed places, posting them by families with their swords, spears and bows" (v. 13). To be forewarned is to be forearmed. A lot of leaders make the mistake of underestimating their opposition. Don't be naive. As Nehemiah observed, "From that day on, half of my men did the work, while the other half were equipped with spears, shields, bows and armor" (v. 16).

This "watch *and* pray" idea occurs throughout the Bible. Not only are we to intercede, but we are also to do everything we can to be prepared for the opposition, in order to protect the church. Good leaders know where they are vulnerable and reinforce that area.

Recast the Vision

When discouragement was greatest, Nehemiah recast the vision by pointing people to God. He says, "After I looked things over, I stood up and said to the nobles, the officials and the rest of the people, 'Don't be afraid of them. Remember the Lord, who is great and awesome, and fight for your brothers, your sons and your daughters, your wives and your homes'" (v. 14).

The Christian's ultimate confidence comes from remembering how great God is. In pointing your people to God, you might say: "God is bigger than this. He is awesome. He has called us to do this. Nothing is impossible with God, Jesus reminds us."

Vision starts with remembering God. With renewed vision comes new courage.

Rally the Troops

Armed with fresh vision, Nehemiah was able to rally the people together to overcome the opposition. "Then I said to the nobles, the officials, and the rest of the people, 'The work is extensive and spread out, and we are widely separated from each other along the wall. Whenever you hear the sound of the trumpet, join us there. Our God will fight for us!'" (v. 19).

God's people standing together, believing Him for the impossible, can do amazing things with His help. Tremendous power is released when God's people are of one heart.

When you challenge people to give it everything they have, joining hands together with God the Holy Spirit, you will receive the power you need to overcome and accomplish what God has called you to do. Renewed vision, like a sounding trumpet, becomes a rally point that reassures the people and leads to victory.

Refuse to Quit

In spite of being threatened with loss of their lives, they refused to quit. "So we continued to work," Nehemiah says (v. 21). They worked through the night. They didn't even leave to go home. When they became tired, they slept in their work clothes.

Though tempted to give up, Nehemiah persisted. Nothing can take the place of "staying on the wall." He kept focused. He stayed true, leading the people in what God had called them to accomplish.

Even when the enemies were hurling their fiercest attack directly at Nehemiah, menacing his life and threatening to discredit him to the king, he was able to reply: "I am carrying on a great project and cannot go down. Why should the work stop while I leave it and go down to you?" (6:3). Nehemiah persisted through every kind of attack, both internal and external.

---

*Let your dreams, not your regrets,
control your life.*

As a result, he broke through to victory. Soon enough, Nehemiah could report that "the wall was completed" (v. 15). Persistence and faith had paid off.

God's people across the Scriptures needed to hear that same message. One of the most-repeated commands from God throughout the Bible is not to be so afraid that you quit. As God told Israel's leadership, when they approached the Promised Land, "Have I not commanded you? Be strong and courageous. Do not be terrified; do not be discouraged, for the LORD your God will be with you wherever you go" (Josh. 1:9).

Opposition comes and goes in waves. The tide may be out right now, but it will come back in. Be true to what God has called you to do.

What do *you* need to do to move forward? What is *your* best response to opposition? What should *you* do when under attack? May God replace your discouragement with new courage. Let your dreams, not your regrets, control your life.

Wouldn't you rather attempt something great for God and fail, than do nothing and succeed? God can accomplish amazing things through men and women who are steadfast, unmovable, always abounding as they do the work of the Lord.

20

HANDLING CRITICISM IN A POSITIVE WAY

The ability to deal with criticism can make us or break us. No one is indifferent to it. In the many leadership roles I've held throughout my life, the most painful and difficult moments have revolved around criticism.

The way to get on top of any negative attack is to take a positive action. It need not defeat your spirit. In fact, criticism can help us grow. Here's what I have learned over the years about turning the negative into the positive.

All Leaders Get Criticized

If you're a leader, you will be criticized. No matter what you do, people will criticize you. The bigger or more public your ministry becomes, the more criticism you'll receive from people you don't even know.

That seems so unjust! Criticism always hurts. It never feels good. As you're trying to do your very best, someone else says something negative that you don't think you deserve. You're trying to be a caring leader, but the more emotionally vulnerable you are, the more deeply the criticism can touch you. It feels painful whether it comes from a longtime church member or from someone you don't know.

I grew up in a denomination where the surest sign of success was a congregation's unanimous vote of support, asking the pastor to stay another year. My first church was one I pioneered. I thought that if I worked hard, loved God, and treated everyone as I would want to be treated, then I would receive a unanimous vote.

When the results of my first vote were announced, I was crushed. The congregation had cast 31 yes votes and 2 no votes. The negative votes put me into depression. I thought I had failed miserably. To add insult to injury, I found out that those who voted no were a middle-age couple whose family I had spent hours helping.

My father, a district superintendent, gave me some wise advice: If you are a leader, you cannot avoid being criticized. It goes with the territory. The more visible and successful leaders are, the more they become a target for unjust and unfair criticism. If you are a person who makes things happen, you will receive derogatory feedback.

Even the best of people get criticized. Jesus, whose motive was always pure and whose character was spotless, was called a glutton (Matt. 11:19), a drunkard (Luke 7:34), a Samaritan (John 8:48), and a friend of sinners (Mark 2:16). Jesus, the perfect one, was criticized unjustly and severely by friends and foes alike.

In many cases, you're not being criticized because of who you are or what you've done, so learn how not to take it personally. Some people would criticize Jesus if he were walking around on earth today.

All Christians, and especially leaders, will receive flak. The real question is, how will you respond to it?

You Always Have More than One Option

My friend John Maxwell tells a story about a critical, negative barber. A salesman came in for a haircut and described his upcoming trip to Rome. The barber had only unpleasant, discouraging comments about his customer's airline choice, hotel, destination, business prospects, and even the man's dream of having an audience with the pope.

Two months later the salesman returned to the barber shop. "It was wonderful," he reported. "The flight was perfect and the hotel service excellent. I made a big sale, and I got to meet the pope!"

"What did he say?" asked the barber.

"He placed his hand on my head," replied the businessman, "and he asked, 'My son, where did you get such a lousy haircut?'"

If my attitude and actions are right before God, then I can be at peace with Him.

In life, what you see is what you get. Nowhere is this more true than in your attitude. Too often we allow someone else's perception to become our reality.

We always have the choice of attitude in how to handle criticism. That choice will make or break us. No matter how negative other people are, it is important to handle criticism in a positive way. I'm not responsible for anyone else's actions or attitudes, only my own. If my attitude and actions are right before God, then I can be at peace with Him. If we don't handle criticism in a correct way, we become victims, not victors. We serve a God who helps us turn bad into good, just as He did with the patriarch Joseph (see Gen. 50:20).

You Can Be Positive

There are only two ways to handle criticism: positively or negatively. The choice is yours. Never surrender your emotional life to negative people or to negative attacks. Live by the higher call, described in the Scriptures as the life of love.

These seven steps show how to handle criticism in a positive manner.

Step 1. Understand the difference between constructive and destructive criticism.

Cynicism is a terrible, growing disease in society today. The cynic in us looks for the worst and finds it. In no other area of life than here do we need more "renewing of [the] mind" (Rom. 12:2).

When criticized, look behind the words and see the spirit of the person. Is the individual trying to help and improve or trying to destroy?

I was in Chicago with the Beeson Institute for Advanced Church Leadership. On one of our days at Willow Creek Community Church, Bill Hybels shared with us that four people evaluate him every time he preaches. These are people he obviously trusts. He knows without a doubt that they care about him personally. This feedback group offers a great example of how constructive criticism can help someone keep growing in excellence in ministry.

Step 2. Determine not to waste energy fighting destructive criticism.

Jesus saw no profit in fighting unjust criticism. After a long and taxing day, Jesus sent His disciples into a village to arrange food and lodging. When the townspeople refused hospitality, the disciples wanted to fight back by calling fire from heaven (see Luke 9:54). Jesus responded by calming the disciples and leading them to the next village.

If an individual or group genuinely wants to help me, then I want to listen and learn all I can. If it's obvious that the motive is self-serving, then I don't put as much value in listening to what they have to say. Although every criticism contains a little bit of truth (see step 5 below), some of the best lessons I've learned have come from people I consider to be critics.

Step 3. Try to understand the source of the criticism.

Someone has said, "Adverse criticism from a wise man is more to be desired than enthusiastic approval of a fool." When Jesus was mocked on the Cross, He prayed, "Father, forgive them, for they do not know what they are doing" (Luke 23:34). He said, in effect, that they simply did not understand the issues involved.

When being criticized, can you place yourself in the other person's shoes? Is this person speaking from wisdom or from a lack of understanding?

Step 4. See if there's a crowd with the critic.

At New Hope Community Church, we used "communication cards" as feedback tools. I would read through them each Sunday, watching for positive comments as well as criticism. If on a given day or month many cards voiced a similar problem, then I knew I had better listen. If only one person raised an issue, I would listen but I would also consider that maybe this person simply had a bad day.

Step 5. Open yourself to see if you can benefit from the criticism.

Heb. 12 says that children of God are at times going to be corrected because God the Father loves us. Admittedly, discipline can be painful. But how else will we grow? Prov. 27:5-6 says, "Better is open rebuke than hidden love. Wounds from a friend can be trusted, but an enemy multiplies kisses."

When criticism comes, ask yourself these questions: "Is there any portion of truth in it?" "Is there any lesson here that God wants me to learn?" Your critics could be your best friends by helping you see blind spots where you need to grow.

After asking these questions and satisfying yourself that no truth lies behind a criticism, then discard it. With God's help, stand up and be the confident person He created you to be. Don't allow yourself to get bogged down by negative people.

Step 6. Seek first to please God more than man.

Cultivate the Mind of Christ, Equipping Yourself to Handle Criticism, by Becoming . . .

Appreciative: "I thank my God every time I remember you" (Phil. 1:3).

Considerate: "If what I eat causes my brother to fall into sin, I will never eat meat again, so that I will not cause him to fall" (1 Cor. 8:13).

Humble: "I am less than the least of all God's people" (Eph. 3:8).

Servantlike: "A servant of Christ Jesus" (Rom. 1:1).

Confident: "I can do all things through Christ who strengthens me" (Phil. 4:13, NKJV).

Courageous: "Fear not, for I have redeemed you; I have summoned you by name; you are mine" (Isa. 43:1).

Excited: "I am convinced that neither death nor life . . . nor anything else in all creation, will be able to separate us from the love of God that is in Christ Jesus our Lord" (Rom. 8:38-39).

A Goal-Setter: After three missionary journeys, "I plan to . . . go to Spain" (Rom. 15:24).

Persistent: "For two whole years Paul stayed there . . . Boldly and without hindrance he preached the kingdom of God and taught about the Lord Jesus Christ" (Acts 28:30-31).

A Positive Thinker: "If God is for us, who can be against us?" (Rom. 8:31).

Victorious: "And the Lord will deliver me from every evil work and preserve me for His heavenly kingdom" (2 Tim. 4:18, NKJV).

I have often wondered how the apostle Paul lived under the pressures of all the criticism he received. Somehow he seemed content, even as he pressed ahead to achieve great projects for God. How? He was concerned primarily with pleasing God. "He that judgeth me is the Lord," he said (1 Cor. 4:4, KJV).

Is absence of criticism a sign that a Christian's life is pleasing to God? Not necessarily. God asks us to trust Him, to obey Him, to say yes to living life His way. If we live with that attitude, then we don't need to take ourselves too seriously. He will take up the slack.

Step 7. When criticized, take positive action instead of being negative and defensive.

A negative attitude toward criticism can become more destructive to you than the criticism itself. The late Herman Heckman, great football coach at Tennessee, Army, and Yale, said, "When you are being run out of town, get to the head of the line and look as though you are leading a parade."

So much of Jesus' Sermon on the Mount (Matt. 5—7) helps us grow in becoming proactive. Bless them . . . pray for them . . . go the extra mile . . . turn the other cheek—these are all commands for positive action.

How you handle criticism is much more important than the criticism itself.

I read a devotional from E. Stanley Jones that reminded me not only to pray *for* my critics but, whenever possible, to pray *with* them. The miracle of prayer changes both people. We become victor instead of victim as we learn to take constructive action instead of reacting in negative ways.

I've also found that when I spend time praying the forgiveness passages of the Lord's Prayer, God builds a bank of grace in me so that I can forgive people almost before they do something that hurts me. When I haven't prepared myself and my "bank account" is low, things get to me. They crawl inside my spirit, gnaw at it, and try to kill me. The mind of Christ is preventive medicine that we can use to prepare ourselves.

In ministry we have to choose and cultivate right attitudes. God calls leaders to higher ground. We want to initiate a good response, not react in kind. Otherwise, when criticism comes, we'll become part of a damaging chain reaction, like those domino-style, multicar accidents where dozens of vehicles crash into each other.

According to 1 Pet. 2, Christ left us an example for times of unjust suffering: "He did not threaten, but committed Himself to Him who judges righteously" (v. 23, NKJV). When you "bless those who persecute you; bless and do not curse" (Rom. 12:14), you will learn to overcome evil with good.

How you handle criticism is much more important than the criticism itself. Today, take every opportunity to do something positive for or toward the person who attacks you or criticizes the ministry you serve.

21

RAISING THE OVERALL SATISFACTION LEVEL IN YOUR CHURCH

How do you make church people happy? As a young pastor I thought my job was to make everyone happy. I often thought that if I could experience one day when everyone was content, I'd be the closest to heaven I'd ever get in this life.

Over the years as I've talked with clergy from other denominations and geographies, I've learned that I was not alone. Most of us enter the ministry with an expectation or desire to be a one-on-one caregiver. As a result, it's easy to fall into the trap of thinking our job is to make everyone feel satisfied.

One day, while reflecting on Exod. 12:17, I realized I can't make people happy. That's their decision. What were the children of Israel doing within days after Moses led them across the Red Sea? Shortly after firsthand participation in this mighty, miraculous act of God, they moaned and cried out, in effect, "I want to go back to Egypt."

As you may have experienced the day after the greatest happening in your church's history, you can always find people who are unhappy. Trying to make people in your parish happy is an impossible task. You can never complete it or win at it.

Sources of Dissatisfaction

Although you and I cannot make individual people happy, we can raise the overall satisfaction level of the church community. Every congregation has a satisfaction level and a dissatisfaction level. These two indicators are always changing. They are like a slippery frog you can never catch.

In the Jethro principles found in Exodus 18, Moses' father-in-law gave advice on how to raise people's sights from grumbling and complaining to a higher level of satisfaction. Moses was in an unhealthy position, trying to solve everyone's problems. His approach to ministry created codependent relationships.

His father-in-law told him, "What you are doing is not good. You and these people who come to you will only wear yourselves out. The work is too heavy for you; you cannot handle it alone" (Exod. 18:17-18). Jethro showed Moses how to mobilize the people and leaders in a pastoral care ratio of 1:10. One guideline for pastoral ministry is: If your span of pastoral care is more than 10 people, you are in trouble or are headed for it.

Raising the "Satisfaction Level"

As Moses decentralized and delegated personal-level ministry, the overall satisfaction level of the children of Israel rose to new heights. The reason stems from the fact that two of our basic needs are for security and significance. Every child of God, both then and now, has these two needs. When you share ministry and develop lay leaders who use their spiritual gifts to care for their span of 10 or so, both these needs are met. Lay leaders then experience the significance and satisfaction of being used of God to their fullest intent and capacity. The people also sense a security through being cared for in community.

One quality I love about small-group ministry is that pastoral care isn't limited to a 1:10 ratio. In reality, as the people grow together in love and community, 10 people care for 10 people.

At New Hope Community Church, where we had 500 trained, dedicated leaders, our lay pastors came to worship services with a high level of satisfaction and fulfillment. The people they were caring for had a sense of belonging and security that increased the satisfaction level of the entire church body.

The Bottom Line of Christian Community

The bottom line is that satisfaction directly results from living in small-group community fellowships within the larger community. It is the result of people caring for one another. It is

Steps Toward Greater Satisfaction

A direct relationship exists between the satisfaction level and the number of people who are involved in ministry. The way to raise it is to get more people involved in ministry. Here are some paths you might pursue:

1. Preach on Spiritual Gifts. In drawing sermon applications, challenge hearers to become involved in a group context that uses their gifts. Distribute spiritual gift inventories and then try to match people with ministries.

2. Create a Ministry Fair. Through booths or other displays, highlight all the ways people can become involved in ministry.

3. Distribute a Permission-Giving Document. Show people the steps by which they can launch new ministries at your church.

4. Sponsor a Super Bowl Weekend. Offer an opportunity to hear testimonies from various small-group participants, to visit a group, or to sign up for becoming a leader in training.

5. Launch a Short-Term Class Designed for Ministry Finding. Combine spiritual-gift inventories and ministry mobilization training into a Sunday School class or short-term seminar.

also the result of being in ministry and using one's spiritual gifts.

The best way to spend time each day is not in trying to make people happy. Rather, set your focus on getting people to discover and use their spiritual gifts. Leadership development is the best priority you can support as a pastor, while at the same time modeling pastoral care for the people under your care.

Setting Satisfaction Goals

How many of your people are actively involved in one or more of your congregation's subunits (group, team, task force, care circle, etc.)?

- 20 percent? The dissatisfaction level is usually quite high in churches like this.
- 40 percent? In churches like this, the pastoral staff persons may be trying to do too much of the caregiving by themselves.
- 60 percent? To achieve greater lay involvement, the pastor must make heroes of lay caregivers.
- 80 percent? At this point, the church may grow, as group members reach out beyond church walls.
- 100 percent? Some of the healthiest churches have more people in groups than in corporate worship!

22

HANDLING SUCCESS SUCCESSFULLY

In 1981, after nine years of wandering from one rented facility to another, New Hope Community Church moved into our first "real" building. One of my mentors, Robert Schuller, came to Portland to serve as our guest speaker. Just before we went to the platform, he looked at me and said, "You'll have to learn how to manage success, and that will be more difficult for you."

I didn't understand what he meant, but I didn't forget what he said. As time went by, his words began to make sense. New Hope's "success" became a challenge. With more visibility in ministry came more respect and influence. Yet each time God blessed the church with further advancement in ministry, I had to deal with new blind spots in my perception. In fact, no matter at what level of ministry I was, the most difficult person to manage has always been me.

The Need for Ego Adjustments

Success in ministry is the next step down the road to where God wants to take you. It is an open gate to greater possibilities. It is a harvest from good seeds sown. Experiencing these results comes from being the best person you can be as Jesus lives through you.

With each new stage of success comes the challenge of a new ego adjustment. For example, when I wrote my first book, it took about six weeks to level out to where anyone else could live with me! I was drowning in a sea of self-grandeur.

Over the years I've enjoyed notoriety and national recognition for being a pacesetter in small-group ministry. The temptation has been to place too much confidence in myself. The truth is that I'm just one of many innovators. Many unknown people are pioneering marvelous ministries with small groups. Even if I were the top dog, it wouldn't be long before someone else came along and took a church beyond today's standard.

I appreciate the perspective shown in a book called *Rethinking the Church*. In it, church planter James Emery White tells the story of Roger Bannister, the athlete who did what everyone said was impossible: He ran a mile in less than four minutes. Yet the very year after that barrier broke, 37 other runners did the same thing. The following year, more than 300 others did so.

White calls Bill Hybels and Rick Warren "the 'Roger Bannisters' of the church world . . . pioneers who have blazed the trail that so many of us have followed" (White 1997, 12). Every leader, even if on center stage in public attention, provides only one thread in the great tapestry God is weaving. In reality, today's successes become outdated paradigms tomorrow. If we're not continuing to learn and move beyond, we'll drop behind.

God can use us only when ego is placed at the Cross.

New achievements also produce stress. People start expecting perfection from a successful ministry. Their expectations rose at New Hope, almost to the point of unreality, since the church's other leaders and I still had weaknesses like everyone else. I still faced the same kinds of problems that all others in ministry experienced. I wanted to live up to a high standard, to be the best person I could be to the glory of God, but it was not easy.

Then about the time I thought I'd arrived in terms of learning to live in this new world, everything changed. Ministry is like a tide; it involves a continual flow of people who come and go. If a leader is not careful, a dangerous attitude can creep in. When you're not getting results, you feel like a failure; when good things are happening, you feel like the cause.

Both attitudes are wrong. Instead, our significance comes from the Lord, whose love is not tied to our performance. "But God demonstrates his own love for us in this: While we were still sinners, Christ died for us" (Rom. 5:8).

God can use us only when ego is placed at the Cross. When our egos inflate, we soon lose our sense of dependence on Him. When that happens, we lose the power for effective ministry. "I have been crucified with Christ and I no longer live, but Christ lives in me. The life I live in the body, I live by faith in the Son of God, who loved me and gave himself for me" (Gal. 2:20).

The relational concept "in Christ" is so important that it occurs almost 100 times in the New Testament. God cares foremost about our hearts: who we are in Him, not merely what we do.

Potholes on the Road to Success

As you experience a new level of success in ministry, at least five different potholes can mess up your journey. Sexual immorality, even if in private, will destroy the bond and trust of a marriage. Imbalance, such as putting work ahead of family, may allow you to reach the top—only to discover that no one is present to share your accomplishments. Abuse of power results in mistreating other people. Greed causes you to be a slave to possessions and money. And forgetting God will lead to self-destruction.

We might appear on the surface to be successful, but if we've fallen into one of these potholes, we're actually going nowhere fast. As the pilot of an airplane announced to his passengers, "Ladies and gentlemen, I have good news and bad news. On the bad side, our instruments have gone out and we don't know where we're going. The good news is that we've picked up a tailwind and are making very good time." Successful people must take care not to self-destruct by thinking their success is their own. Success in ministry is always a generous gift of God.

The best way to handle error is to turn squarely in the right way, repenting if necessary. This means we are sick of sin and defeat and are going to change with God's help. We want Christ to turn our past failures into stepping-stones to future success.

The road to failure is paved with good intentions. We gain the road to success by letting Jesus Christ become Lord. As the Scripture promises, "The one who is in you is greater than the one who is in the world" (1 John 4:4).

Life's greatest challenge is to be God's person.

Keep learning what is right and doing it. When you make right decisions and do what's right and plant good seeds, you reap good results. Continued success results from continued improvement. Successful people look to the Word of God, learn what is right, and live in faith and obedience. Prov. 3:21 says, "Have two goals: wisdom—that is, knowing and doing right—and common sense" (TLB). If you do this, you will have a successful and prosperous life.

See big and go for it. Life's greatest challenge is to be God's person. Be the instrument and steward of the many gifts God has placed in you. Then handle the resultant success by doing all to the glory of God.

The Fine Line Between Conceit and Confidence

We fulfill our destiny when Christ is first. We flounder whenever we put ourselves ahead of Christ or others. Is it possible to have confidence without conceit? Jesus is the perfect example. He knew who He was, yet He lived as a servant.

The worst thing you can do is put stock in your own press clippings. Each time breakthroughs occur in your ministry, it's important to remember that success is an unending journey.

When we become protective or exclusive, our accomplishments tend to fade away and die. The only ministry we have is when we're servants.

A couple of years before I left New Hope to come to the Beeson Center, the Holy Spirit spoke to me that my name was being recognized first in Portland, and the name New Hope Community Church was second in public awareness. God began to show me that I needed to decrease and the church to increase. That attitude made a successful transition possible when I left.

A book by John Maxwell, *The Success Journey* (1997), affirms the truth that success is a lifelong process. I saw a great illustration of that perspective in my friend Elmer Towns. He's a respected leader who has written dozens of books and hundreds of magazine articles. He is the cofounder of a major university. Yet when he phoned me on his 65th birthday, he told me his thoughts of enrolling in a new degree program, just to keep learning and growing.

I want to be like that! Elmer Towns doesn't rest on his laurels. Instead, he moves on to the next place. People like him are the best models of how to handle success. They take seriously their responsibility to keep moving forward.

EPILOGUE

You and I increase our leadership influence as we practice humility. International evangelist Luis Palau once told me a story from a time he was overseas with Billy Graham in a crusade. A young pastor kept coming to Graham's hotel, asking to meet personally with the great evangelist. The crusade staff politely explained each time that they were sorry not to be able to grant the request.

One day the young man was making his appeal and Billy Graham happened to be walking through the lobby. "Bring him up to the room," Graham instructed his staff.

When the pastor was seated, Graham caringly asked, "What can I do for you, son?"

"Dr. Graham," he replied. "Would you put your hands on my head and pray for me that I'd have the anointing of God to reach people in my city for Jesus?"

In response, Graham laid down on the floor, prostrating himself before the Lord. In an attitude that made clear it was God's blessing, not Graham's, that would make any difference, he began to pray. He humbly asked that this young man would be anointed of God and would lead many souls to faith in Jesus Christ so that God may be glorified.

May you multiply your ministry by becoming a leader of leaders.

Luis Palau's point in telling this story is that Billy Graham clearly remembers whose servant he is. For Billy Graham, the only reason to influence others is for the glory of God.

We can all learn from that model. I want to be faithful in how I use my influence to accomplish what God wants done. As a leader I have a stewardship before God for how I gain influence and for what I do with the influence God grants and increases in my life over the years. You do too.

May you and I, through the right motivation, take courage to do in Jesus' name what needs to be done to make a real difference in this world, for now and all eternity. May you multiply your ministry by becoming a leader of leaders.

Whatever you do, give God the glory. As the earliest disciples desired, may "the name of our Lord Jesus . . . be glorified in you, and you in him, according to the grace of our God and the Lord Jesus Christ" (2 Thess. 1:12).

About the Authors

Dr. Dale E. Galloway, over the course of three decades, has pastored four congregations—two new churches and two established churches. He received international recognition for building one of America's great churches, New Hope Community Church in Portland, Oregon, such as receiving the Church of the Year award from *Guidepost Magazine.* As this pacesetting, innovative congregation grew to 6,400 members, he developed hundreds of lay pastors who reached and discipled thousands of unchurched people. Pastors from all over the world came to New Hope's Church Growth Institute to learn how to create and sustain effective cell-group ministries.

In 1995, when Dale accepted the call to his present ministry, New Hope had 500 lay pastors ministering to the church's 5,000-plus small-group members. He now serves as dean of the Beeson International Center for Biblical Preaching and Church Leadership and of the Beeson Institute for Advanced Church Leadership, both based at Asbury Theological Seminary, Wilmore, Kentucky, where he trains pastors to become leaders of leaders—of leaders. He is also a popular speaker at seminars, conferences, and retreats. Dale is the author of 17 books, with more than half a million copies in print, including *Building Teams in Ministry, Making Church Relevant,* and *Leading with Vision.*

Warren Bird assists Dale Galloway in the administration of the Beeson Institute for Advanced Church Leadership. He is also on staff with a growing, innovative church in Princeton, New Jersey. He has coauthored or edited 10 books and more than 100 magazine articles on topics of church trends, church health, and small groups.

Bibliography

Arn, W. Charles. 1997. *How to Start a New Service.* Grand Rapids: Baker.

Barna, George. 1992. *The Power of Vision.* Ventura, Calif.: Gospel Light.

Barnett, Tommy. 1997. *Multiplication.* Lake Mary, Fla.: Creation House.

Berguson, Johnny, with Warren Bird. 1997. *The Comprehensive Guide to Cassette Ministry.* Mansfield, Pa.: Kingdom.

Blanchard, Ken, and Terry Waghorn. 1999. *Mission Possible: Becoming a World-Class Organization While There's Still Time.* New York: McGraw-Hill.

Bramson, Robert M. 1988. *Coping with Difficult People.* New York: Dell.

Bugbee, Bruce, Don Cousins, and Bill Hybels. 1994. *Network Participant's Guide.* Grand Rapids: Zondervan.

Carnegie, Dale. 1936, 1998. *How to Win Friends and Influence People.* New York: Simon and Schuster; 1936; New York: Pocket Books.

Cloud, Henry, and John Townsend. 1996. *The Mom Factor.* Grand Rapids: Zondervan.

Coleman, Robert. 1963, 30th anniversary edition 1993. *The Master Plan of Evangelism.* Grand Rapids: Revell.

Cox, Allan. 1992. *Straight Talk for Monday Morning.* New York: Wiley, John, and Sons.

Drucker, Peter. 1993. *The Effective Executive.* San Francisco: HarperCollins.

"Fix Your Gaze: An Interview with Lon Solomon," *Leadership*, Summer 2000.

Galloway, Dale E. 1980, 1984. *Dare to Discipline Yourself.* Grand Rapids: Revell.

———. *20/20 Vision.* 1986. Portland, Oreg.: Scott Publishing Co.

Galloway, Dale, with Kathi Mills. 1995. *The Small Group Book.* Grand Rapids: Revell.

George, Carl. 1993. *How to Break Growth Barriers.* Grand Rapids: Baker.

Halverson, Richard. 1994. *The Living Body.* Sisters, Oreg.: Multnomah.

Hunter, George. 1996. *Church for the Unchurched.* Nashville: Abingdon.

Hunter, James. 1998. *The Servant.* Roseville, Calif.: Prima Publishing.

Hybels, Bill, and Mark Mittelberg. 1994. *Becoming a Contagious Christian.* Grand Rapids: Zondervan.

———. 2000. *Building a Contagious Church.* Grand Rapids: Zondervan.

Jones, Laurie Beth. 1996. *Jesus CEO.* New York: Hyperion.

Levine, Stuart R. 1993. *The Leader in You.* Crofton, Md.: Poseidon Press.

Maxwell, John. 1997. *The Success Journey.* Atlanta: Maxwell Motivation.

Mead, Loren. 1993. *The Once and Future Church.* Washington, D.C.: Alban Institute.

NetFax No. 86, 12/8/97.

Price, Reynolds. "Jesus of Nazareth." *Time* 154, No. 23 (December 6, 1999) [on-line] [<http://www.time.com/time/magazine/articles/0,3266,35079,00.html>.]

Schaller, Lyle. 1995. *The Small Membership Church: Scenarios for Tomorrow.* Nashville: Abingdon.

Schuller, Robert. 1994 (re-issue). *Peak-to-Peek Principle.* New York: Jove Publications.

Sjogren, Steve. 1993. *Conspiracy of Kindness.* Ann Arbor, Mich.: Vine.

Warren, Rick. 1995. *The Purpose-Driven Church.* Grand Rapids: Zondervan.

White, James Emery. 1997. *Rethinking the Church.* Grand Rapids: Baker Book House.